JUMP STARTS AND SOFT LANDINGS

By Steve Sheely

Jump Starts and Soft Landings is intended for use by your entire group. For activities which instruct participants to "write in their booklet," each member should have their own book or a photocopy of the activity.

Permission given to copy art work for church brochures, fliers, etc. for noncommercial use within your church.

JUMP STARTS AND SOFT LANDINGS

By Steve Sheely

101 more ways to kick off and end meetings

SERENDIPITY / Nashville, TN
1-800-525-9563 / www.serendipityhouse.com
03 04 05 06 07 08 / 10 9 8 7 6

Introduction

Welcome to *Jump Starts and Soft Landings*! This book contains everything you need to turn any meeting into a wonderful time of fun and friendship. *Jump Starts and Soft Landings* will help you take advantage of any occasion when people are gathered together. Simply use the activities in this book to begin and end your meeting and watch your group become a community!

Use these activities for any meeting at your church:

Small Groups
Youth Meetings
New Member Classes
Sunday School
Recovery and AA Groups
Committee Meetings
Retreats
Men's and Women's Groups
Prayer Meetings
Church Staff, Elders, Deacons, Session or Board Meetings
... and many more!

This book is a sequel to *Ice-Breakers and Heart-Warmers* and includes all new activities. Each activity can be identified by symbols running across the top of the page. You can choose activities which match the topic of your meeting or have an entire meeting of nothing but *Jump Starts and Soft Landings*! Avoid getting in a rut and add some pizazz to your meeting!

With *Jump Starts and Soft Landings* your group can become a wonderful place of trust, growth and compassion ... and even a few laughs! So hook up the electrodes, pull the rip cord and let the fun begin!

ANNOUNCING

JUMP
STARTS
AND
SOFT
LANDINGS

Table of Contents

JUMP STARTS

SOFT LANDINGS

What Are Jump Starts and Soft Landings?

Jump Starts get the group off to a good start. Instead of moving immediately into the study and discussion of your group's topic, using a Jump Start helps everyone prepare for the meeting. It provides a fun and interesting way for people to learn more about each other and encourages everyone to talk in a lively, nonthreatening way. Jump Starts help people move out of the business of the day and begin the exciting task of small group conversation.

Imagine your relationships as a house full of rooms. Most day-to-day relationships only visit a few of the rooms. We share information, we talk about the weather, we discuss a purchase, etc. The relationships in a church group can offer much more than that. A healthy group allows each member to bring more of themselves into the safety of Christian fellowship. An effective group should open doors to many rooms, such as playfulness, accountability, prayer, confession, encouragement, affirmation, reminiscing and dreaming.

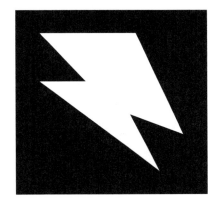

Beginning your group meeting with a Jump Start encourages this process. It creates an opportunity for sharing those parts of ourselves we normally keep locked up, and opens doors which remain shut during the day. Jump Starts begin an important process that enables your small group to be a place where you can let down your guard and be yourself.

During a meeting something special should gradually happen. From the time the group gathers to the time they dismiss, a certain magic should occur. Hopefully, by the time the group is ready to close with prayer, the group has become a safe, trusting community. This process, of course, does not happen by accident.

The Jump Start gets the "community ball" rolling. Bible study and discussion should continue the momentum, moving toward opportunities for personal response to the Scripture and the topic. The prayer time should be the culmination of the community building for each meeting. This is a special time, under God's protection, for the group to share their concerns, express gratitude to God, and pray for each other. If the group has moved through the "trust process" during the course of the meeting, the prayer time should be a powerful spiritual experience.

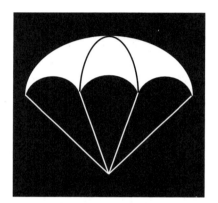

That is why Soft Landings are included in this book. If opening a meeting properly is important, ending a meeting is even more important. Soft Landings are closing activities which help a group capitalize on their time together. Be careful not to lose track of time and miss the wonderful opportunities for the blessings that a Soft Landing can provide!

Soft Landings come in many shapes and sizes. This book includes dozens of ways a Christian small group can close their meeting in prayer. Affirmation exercises, action plans and Scripture promises are also powerful closing activities. Each group should choose the Soft Landing which is best suited for them.

One book cannot include the content for every group meeting at your church. There are thousands of different types of groups, each having different forums for study and discussion. However, one book can contain a collection of Jump Starts and Soft Landings which any small group can use.

Bible study and discussion alone will not necessarily bring a group to a safe place of trust and intimacy. Building a safe, Christian community is a powerful experience, but it is also a delicate process. With an appropriate Jump Start and Soft Landing, a group can be a special place where people can pray, weep, laugh, confess, encourage and even apply Scripture to their lives.

Choosing the Right
Jump Start and Soft Landing

How do you decide which Jump Start or Soft Landing to use for your meeting? Choosing an appropriate Jump Start or Soft Landing for your group is easy. Use the different symbols to help you identify the correct activity for your group. You can find these symbols along the top of each page.

Is an exercise a Jump Start or a Soft Landing?
The first symbol on each page tells you if the exercise is a Jump Start or a Soft Landing. Remember, be sure to leave enough time for the Soft Landing! These moments can be the most precious part of your meeting! The two symbols are:

Jump Start

Soft Landing

How long has the group been together?
The second symbol on each page tells you if the Jump Start or Soft Landing should be used with a new group, an adolescent group, a mature group or a group that has decided to end:

New Group

6 weeks to 3 months

Mature Group (over 3 months)

Group that has decided to end

Generally speaking, Jump Starts and Soft Landings for newer groups will invite less disclosure and risk than more mature groups. Groups that have decided to end also need special help to close their group properly. Activities with none of these four icons can be used with any group.

What is the topic of your meeting?

Matching the topic of the Jump Start and Soft Landing with the topic of the current discussion can make the small group meeting more meaningful for everyone. Look for the following symbols which identify the topics of the Jump Starts and Soft Landings. Some Jump Starts and Soft Landings will have more than one of these symbols:

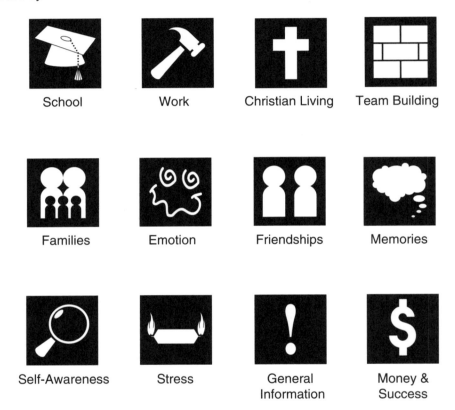

| School | Work | Christian Living | Team Building |

| Families | Emotion | Friendships | Memories |

| Self-Awareness | Stress | General Information | Money & Success |

You can also choose Jump Starts and Soft Landings for large groups, or groups that might need a fun or serious activity.

| Large groups | Fun | Serious |

Soft Landings might have some different topics, such as:

Prayer

Bible
Promises

Ministry &
Service

Affirmation

What type of event will the Jump Start or Soft Landing be used for?

What event you are having will help you determine which Jump Start or Soft Landing you use. For example, a youth retreat might require a different "get acquainted!" activity than a meeting of the elders. For more information about using different Jump Starts and Soft Landings at various church events, see pages 19–21.

Women's
Group

New Member
Class

Retreat

Recovery /
AA

Youth

Prayer Meetings /
Church Supper

Singles

Outreach

Leadership
Teams /
Committees

Men's Groups

Family Groups

Couples /
Marriage

Jump Starts and Soft Landings for 12 Different Church Events

The people in your church are its greatest resource and richest treasure. But how often do meetings focus on learning, decision-making and programming, without ever learning anything about the person sitting next to us? Jump Starts and Soft Landings can help people connect, regardless of the purpose of the gathering.

Depending on your event, the following suggestions will help you choose a Jump Start and a Soft Landing.

> New Member Classes
> Leadership Teams, Ministry Teams and Committees
> Recovery and 12-Step Groups
> Retreats
> Men's Groups
> Youth Meetings
> Prayer Meetings and Church Suppers
> Singles Groups
> Women's Groups
> Couples / Marriage Classes
> Family and Intergenerational Events
> Outreach Activities

New Member Classes
These Jump Starts and Soft Landings are recommended for your New Member Classes. Try to imagine what you would like your new members to experience before they become active church members.

"Prayer Methods," (p. 92)   "Church Bingo," (p. 80)
"Life Map," (p. 72)   "Spiritual Journey," (p. 67)

Leadership Teams, Ministry Teams and Committees
When the church staff, elders, deacons, session, church board or other church leaders gather for a meeting, use Jump Starts and Soft Landings to demonstrate the importance of personal contact.

"Group Machine," (p. 90)   "Group Affirmation" (p. 114)
"C.E.O." (p. 106)   "Body of Christ" (p.111)

Recovery and 12-Step Groups

Support and Recovery Groups frequently focus on self-awareness and include opportunities for sharing at a greater depth. Remember to give each person the option of "passing" if they do not want to answer.

"How I Feel About this Group" (p. 24)   "Healthy Goals" (p. 64)
"State of Mind" (p. 35)   "Coping Skills" (p. 77)
"Open Your Present" (p. 76)

Retreats

When church folks get away for a weekend and let their hair down, watch out! Retreats are a great opportunity for people to get better acquainted and make marvelous new friends.

"Activity Bingo" (p. 86)   "Knots" (p. 82)
"How to Form a Group" (p. 84)   "Who Am I?" (p. 83)

Men's Groups

Do not underestimate the capacity for men to take advantage of an opportunity to talk about their lives and faith. Jump Starts and Soft Landings can help a men's group have a more meaningful meeting.

"If Today Was A ..." (p. 81)   "Hobbies & Skills" (p. 31)
"The Great Outdoors" (p. 32)   "The Perfect Job" (p. 54)
"My Job Is Like ..." (p. 52)   "Life Map" (p. 72)

Youth Meetings

Young people love to talk about themselves and usually find controlled disclosure deeply satisfying. Learning about one another and affirming one another is a great way to discourage insults and cliques.

"Activity Bingo" (p. 86)   "Groovy Grandparents" (p. 48)
"My School Is Like ..." (p. 53)   "Relationshps Wanted" (p. 70)
"Crazy Ovations" (p. 122)   "God's Will" (p. 115)

Prayer Meetings and Church Suppers

Many churches continue to enjoy weeknight prayer meetings, often following a church dinner. The right Jump Start or Soft Landing can help these meetings become even more special.

"Church Bingo" (p. 80)   "Name Game" (p. 25)
"Spiritual Inventory" (p. 42)   "The 'One Anothers' " (p. 43)
"Life Map" (p. 72)   "Prayer Form" (p. 94)

Singles Groups

Jump Starts and Soft Landings can be a tremendous contribution to the social needs and interests of single adults, and they can also be used to help these groups move comfortably toward community.

"Press Conference" (p. 27)   "Famous Firsts" (p. 40)
"Spiritual Inventory" (p. 42)   "Relationships Wanted" (p. 70)
"My Job Is Like ..." (p. 52)   "Self–Scale" (p. 36)

Women's Groups

Any women's event, from a Bible study to a fashion show can be an opportunity for people to move beyond "everyday" conversation to the kind of communication available to church members.

"I Want To Learn ..." (p. 33)   "Name Game" (p. 25)
"Family Classics" (p. 38)   "I Am Like This Object ..." (p. 57)
"Relax!" (p. 50)

Couple's and Marriage Classes

Take advantage of the opportunity to use Jump Starts and Soft Landings which help married couples open up in a way that will benefit them both as individuals and couples.

"The Great Outdoors" (p. 32)   "Let's Choose a Topic" (p. 30)
"My ABC's" (p. 39)   "Time Will Tell" (p. 44)

Family and Intergenerational Events

Events for people of different generations are as rewarding as they are challenging. Fortunately, we all have more in common than we might suspect.

"Activity Bingo" (p. 86)   "Face the Facts" (p. 46)
"I Want To Learn" (p. 33)   "Family Classics" (p. 38)
"Famous Firsts" (p. 40)   "Whispers" (p. 37)

Outreach Activities

Special care must be taken anytime nonmembers are invited to a church function. Participants should be encouraged to get acquainted and make new friends, without concern about embarrassment.

"Who Am I"? (p. 83)   "Hobbies and Skills" (p. 31)
"Famous Firsts" (p. 40)   "If Today Was A ..." (p. 81)

Helpful Hints and Terrific Tips

Here are some hints which will help you make the most out of this book:

1. Each group member should feel free to elaborate on his or her responses to the Jump Starts and Soft Landings.

2. The leader might begin the Jump Start or Soft Landing with instructions about time, such as "We have enough time for each person to talk about their answers for three minutes."

3. Feel free to "pass" at any time if you do not want to talk.

4. You might need to adapt or change a Jump Start or Soft Landing to fit the specific needs of your group. Be creative!

5. Feel free to use the same Jump Start or Soft Landing more than once. Sometimes answers will change in interesting ways!

6. You might wish to use several Jump Starts or Soft Landings of a similar topic for an entire meeting!

7. Certain Jump Starts and Soft Landings could be connected, using a particular Jump Start with a matching Soft Landing.

8. Look for the at the bottom of the page of some Jump Starts. The parachute indicates ideas for making a Soft Landing out of that particular Jump Start. For example, if the Jump Start is about time management, the might suggest ending your meeting by praying about the different tasks in your life.

9. Use extra care when using Jump Starts and Soft Landings in certain support groups, recovery groups, shame-based groups or other sensitive-issue groups. Some of the Jump Starts and Soft Landings ask questions about families, relationships, past experiences, etc. which might be difficult for some people to answer freely.

10. Use a variety of Jump Starts and Soft Landings. This will help people express different feelings, memories, dreams and ideas.

11. Sometimes the group leader will need to be the "guinea pig." This means that the group leader should be the first one to try a particular Jump Start or Soft Landing.

12. For meetings which include Bible study and discussion, use the following principles:

Include discussion questions which gradually allow for more and more personal disclosure.

Avoid discussion questions which require only "right or wrong" answers. Ask open-ended questions which give people the freedom to answer from their personal experience.

For a new group and during the beginning of the discussion time, ask questions with multiple-choice options so everyone, no matter how much they know about the Bible, can answer without being embarrassed.

13. If time is a problem or if the group seems a little "shy," divide into foursomes so your group members can talk openly without being intimidated by talking in front of the entire group.

14. Strive for a balanced group, which includes Bible study, group building, outreach and some kind of ministry project.

15. Use a group covenant like the one on page 91.

16. Encourage your group members to avoid unsolicited judging, advice giving, and problem solving. Though offered with the best of intentions, this kind of behavior can kill a group.

How I Feel About This Group

How do you feel about being in this group? Choose a picture below which best describes your thoughts on being in this group. Then go around the room and take turns sharing what you have chosen. (This Jump Start is from the small group guide to Howard E. Butt's *Renewing America's Soul*, by Steve Sheely. Used with permission.)

Dried-up Plant
I'm ready for a shower of renewal from this group.

Key Witness
I feel like I'm about to be cross-examined.

Statue
I'm afraid everyone is not going to like the real me.

Paratrooper
I'm a little anxious because I'm not sure where we're going to land.

Turtle
I'll come out of my shell if it is safe.

Clown
I'm going to act funny at first so no one knows how I feel.

Pirate
I'm hoping to find treasure here!

Fluttering Moth
I'm drawn to the light and warmth this group will provide.

News Helicopter
I think I'll hover at a distance and see what happens.

Name Game

Your name says a lot about you. This Jump Start will help your group get to know you better. Write your first and last name in the spaces below, beginning with the first letter of your first name and ending with the last letter of your last name. Then choose a word from each category that begins with those letters. Take turns telling your group your name and the words you chose.

_____ One of my favorite foods that begins with this letter is:

_____ One thing I do for fun that starts with this letter is:

_____ A quality about my work habits that starts with this letter is:

_____ A place I've been that begins with this letter is:

_____ A friend or acquaintance whose first name starts with this letter is:

_____ A plant or animal I like that starts with this letter is:

_____ A sports or entertainment celebrity I admire whose name starts with this letter is:

_____ A positive quality about me that comes out in my friendships that starts with this letter is:

_____ A book or magazine I have enjoyed that begins with this letter is:

_____ A song I like that begins with this letter is:

_____ Something I would rather not do in my spare time that starts with this letter is:

_____ A favorite possession I own that starts with this letter is:

_____ A word that best describes my sense of humor that begins with this letter is:

_____ A physical feature about myself that I especially like that starts with this letter is:

_____ A place I would never want to visit on a vacation that begins with this letter is:

_____ A movie or television show I enjoy that starts with this letter is:

_____ A store or company that I enjoy patronizing that begins with this letter is:

Let Your Fingers Do the Walking

This is a fun, silly game a group can play to help them get acquainted and have a laugh. Everyone stands around a table and uses their "fingers" to walk around the table. Then the group acts out some of the different situations listed below. For example, if the group chooses the circus, each person pretends their fingers are different circus characters, such as clowns, trapeze artists, lion tamers, human cannonball, etc. Have fun!

Ice Capades	Baseball Game
Circus	Square Dance
Hockey Game	Fashion Show
Olympics	Parade
K-Mart Blue Light Special	Carnival
Wedding	Old West Saloon
Earthquake	Church Service
School Dance	Football Game
Ballet	Horse Race

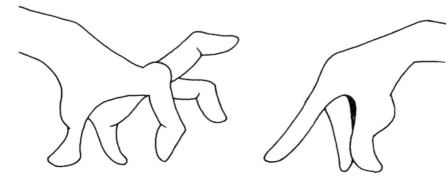

Press Conference

This is a great activity for a new group or when new people are joining an established group. Get in pairs and take turns answering the following questions:

1. What is your name?

2. What do you do to stay busy (job, school, etc.)?

3. Describe your family when you were 7 years old.

4. What was your favorite movie within the last year?

5. Why are you at this meeting?

Gather the group back together. Someone goes first and says their name. Then the group asks that person three questions from the ones listed below, but instead of answering for themselves, the person who interviewed them must answer on their behalf. After the interviewer answers the three questions, the person they interviewed tells how well they did.

1. If this person could vacation anywhere in the world, where would they go?

2. If this person was lost, what would they do?

3. What are this person's hobbies?

4. What is this person's favorite TV show?

5. What is this person's favorite ice cream flavor?

6. What is this person's favorite holiday?

7. What is this person's favorite type of food?

8. What qualities does this person look for in a friend?

Bible Questionnaire

What would you like to know about the Bible? This Jump Start can be used to help a group determine what part of the Bible they want to study, or it can be used to simply learn more about one another. Mark the topics that you would like to learn more about, then rank the ones you marked "1st," "2nd" and "3rd."

_____ How the Bible came to be

_____ An overview of God's plan from Genesis to Revelation

_____ The Old Testament in general

_____ The book of Genesis (Adam and Eve, Abraham, Noah's Ark ...)

_____ Moses, the Egyptians and the Ten Commandments
- ❑ Exodus
- ❑ Leviticus
- ❑ Numbers
- ❑ Deuteronomy
- ❑ Joshua

_____ Samuel, Samson and the time of the Judges
- ❑ Judges
- ❑ Ruth

_____ The Kings, like David, Saul and Solomon
- ❑ 1 and 2 Kings
- ❑ 1 and 2 Chronicles

_____ The Major Prophets, like Isaiah, Ezekiel and Jeremiah
- ❑ Isaiah
- ❑ Ezekiel
- ❑ Jeremiah and Lamentations
- ❑ Daniel

_____ The 12 "minor" prophets
- ❑ Hosea
- ❑ Obadiah
- ❑ Nahum
- ❑ Haggai
- ❑ Joel
- ❑ Jonah
- ❑ Habakkuk
- ❑ Zechariah
- ❑ Amos
- ❑ Micah
- ❑ Zephaniah
- ❑ Malachi

_____ Job, whose faith was tested in times of trouble.

_____ The poetry of the Old Testament
- ❑ Psalms
- ❑ Ecclesiastes
- ❑ Proverbs
- ❑ The Song of Songs

_____ The story of the exile, the return and rebuilding of the temple
❐ Ezra   ❐ Nehemiah

_____ The Apocrypha

_____ The time in between the Old and New Testaments

_____ An overview of the New Testament

_____ The life of Christ (Matthew, Mark, Luke and John)
❐ His teachings and parables
❐ The miracles
❐ The meaning of his death and resurrection

_____ The Gospels (the "good news" about Jesus life, death and resurrection)
❐ Matthew   ❐ Luke
❐ Mark   ❐ John

_____ The differences and similarities of the four Gospels (Matthew, Mark, Luke and John)

_____ What happened to the disciples after Jesus was resurrected (The Acts of the Apostles)

_____ Paul's letters to various churches in the Roman Empire
❐ Romans   ❐ 1 and 2 Corinthians   ❐ Galatians
❐ Ephesians   ❐ Philippians   ❐ Colossians
❐ 1 and 2 Thessalonians

_____ Paul's letters to his friends and proteges
❐ 1 and 2 Timothy   ❐ Titus   ❐ Philemon

_____ The letters of Peter, James, John and Jude
❐ 1 and 2 Peter   ❐ James
❐ 1, 2 and 3 John   ❐ Jude

_____ The good news about Jesus explained to a Jewish audience (Hebrews)

_____ John's vision of the end of time (The Revelation)

Let's Choose a Topic

This Jump Start is similar to the "Bible Questionnaire" on pages 28–29. If your group needs help choosing a study topic, use the list below to come up with ideas. After everyone has marked their preferences, discuss what has been chosen. You might also wish to rank your answers.

I AM MOST INTERESTED IN:

PERSONAL GROWTH AND SELF-AWARENESS

- ❐ Self-esteem
- ❐ Job Issues
- ❐ Relationships
- ❐ Being Single
- ❐ Men's Issues
- ❐ Money
- ❐ Goals and Dreams
- ❐ Sex
- ❐ Communication
- ❐ Health Issues
- ❐ Parenting
- ❐ Marriage
- ❐ Women's Issues
- ❐ Personality Awareness
- ❐ Time Management
- ❐ other:_____

DISCIPLESHIP AND CHRISTIAN LIVING

- ❐ Prayer
- ❐ Ethics and Values
- ❐ Basic Christian Beliefs
- ❐ Spiritual Gifts
- ❐ Personal Holiness
- ❐ Christian Community
- ❐ Spiritual Warfare
- ❐ Holy Spirit
- ❐ Heaven / Eternal LIfe
- ❐ Evangelism and Missions
- ❐ Scripture Memory
- ❐ Serving Others
- ❐ Denominational History
- ❐ Writing a Journal
- ❐ Quiet Time
- ❐ Attributes of God
- ❐ Angels
- ❐ Living Thankfully
- ❐ Everyday Faith
- ❐ other:_____

SUPPORT AND RECOVERY

- ❐ Grief and Loss
- ❐ Overcoming Addiction
- ❐ Healing the Past
- ❐ Weight Loss
- ❐ Parenting Special Kids
- ❐ Blended Families
- ❐ Abuse Recovery
- ❐ Parenting Alone
- ❐ Forgiveness
- ❐ Stress
- ❐ Divorce
- ❐ Couples Without Kids
- ❐ Widows and Widowers
- ❐ Unemployment
- ❐ Midlife Issues
- ❐ Eating Disorders
- ❐ Codependency
- ❐ other:_____

Hobbies and Skills

What are you good at? What special skills and abilities do you have? What would you like to learn? What do you know how to do but don't enjoy doing? Help your group get to know you better by sharing all your various talents, skills and hobbies.

Sewing	Pharmaceuticals	Masonry	Pet shows
Accounting	Music	Welding	Bird watching
Gardening	Audio-Visual	Archery	Weather
Painting	equipment	Magic	Martial arts
Billiards	Child care	Engraving	Disc jockey
Bowling	Graphics design	Plumbing	Psychology
Aerobics	Computer skills	Pest control	Medicine
Model building	History	Scuba diving	Rollerblading
Aquariums	Makeup	Snorkeling	Customer service
Juggling	Costumes	Knitting	Jogging
Home renovation	Drama	Journalism	Swimming
Accounting	Fundraising	Navigator	Cycling
Glassblowing	Marketing	Foreign	Public relations
Embroidery	Publicity	languages	Project managing
Show jumping	Advertising	Archaeology	Budgets
Car racing	Interior design	Library science	Shoe repair
Astronomy	Cooking	Law	Lawn care
Engineering	Skydiving	Biology	Statistics
Finance	Typing	Chemistry	Purchasing
Software	Writing	Genealogy	Banking
Construction	Editing	Oceanography	Delivery
Hydraulics	Human resources	Forestry	Carpentry
Sailing	Fire fighting	Caving	Office manager
Garage saling	Safety	Collecting	Insurance
Flower arranging	Architecture	Antiquing	Hiking
Petroleum	Reading	Physics	Mountain climbing
exploration	Traveling	Recordkeeping	Rafting
Speed reading	Dancing	Data entry	Team sports
Nursing	Electrical wiring	Law enforcement	Weight lifting
Flying	Concrete	Printing	Organizing
Physical therapy	Car repair	Photography	Hunting
Radiology	Upholstery	Skiing	Fishing
Social work	Jewelry making	Snowmobiling	Camping
Counseling	Crafts	Acrobatics	Other:

The Great Outdoors

This Jump Start will help your group get better acquainted and it can help a group decide what they want to do as an outing. Take turns telling the group your favorite outdoor activities, which ones you would like to do and which one the group should do together.

- ❑ hiking
- ❑ camping
- ❑ boating
- ❑ water skiing
- ❑ sailing
- ❑ snowboarding
- ❑ hang gliding
- ❑ ballooning
- ❑ golf
- ❑ snow skiing
- ❑ tennis
- ❑ volleyball
- ❑ frisbee
- ❑ neighborhood walks
- ❑ jogging
- ❑ hunting
- ❑ fishing
- ❑ skeet shooting
- ❑ beachcombing
- ❑ cycling
- ❑ swimming
- ❑ surfing
- ❑ gardening

- ❑ mini golf
- ❑ picnics
- ❑ horseshoes
- ❑ campfires
- ❑ playground
- ❑ amusement parks
- ❑ nature photography
- ❑ caving
- ❑ scuba diving
- ❑ rafting
- ❑ stargazing
- ❑ canoeing
- ❑ butterfly catching
- ❑ snorkeling
- ❑ kayaking
- ❑ mountain biking
- ❑ rowing
- ❑ four-wheeling
- ❑ fossil hunting
- ❑ treasure hunting
- ❑ suntanning
- ❑ snowshoeing
- ❑ sand castle building

I Want to Learn ...

Self-improvement is a continual process. What would you like to learn? If you could take a class and learn how to do anything, what would you choose? Use the list below for ideas, then take turns sharing your response with the group.

I WANT TO LEARN HOW TO:

use a computer
hit a golf ball over 250 yards
surf the net
use a potter's wheel
give someone a great massage
kick a field goal
set the clock on my VCR
parallel park
fight city hall
speak another language like a diplomat
create and follow a budget
run my own business
build a laser beam
read the Bible in the original language
grow orchids
train my dog
ride a unicycle
rip a gnarly Husker-Du
shoot a gun safely
be a human cannonball
fly a plane
work on my own car
dance, dance, dance
give a great toast at a banquet
sail a yacht
run my own farm
be a politician
make movies
discover an undiscovered star or planet
take really great pictures
set the table correctly
complete the *New York Times*
   crossword puzzle
pull in my driveway without running
   over the sprinkler

make my own donuts
play contract bridge
trace my family history
be a great teacher
ride a motorcycle
play a musical instrument
grow an herb garden
be more earth-friendly
order a great bottle of wine
make candles
raise bees and make honey
milk a cow
clap with one hand
catch a really big fish
restore a classic car
ice-skate
ride a horse
carve a turkey
play cricket
design a tall skyscraper
be a great parent
share my feelings
make homemade ice cream
throw things away
build a treehouse
patent and market an invention
deal with the IRS
dig half a hole
build a house
investigate a hot news story
make mud pies
fly a kite
give my cat a bath without getting
   fur on my tongue

The Ideal Group

What does the ideal group look like to you? This is a great Jump Start for getting acquainted, and it can also be used to help a group discuss their experiences for the group. Mark your preferences with an **"X"** below and then take turns comparing your answers.

IN MY OPINION, THE IDEAL GROUP:

has a predictable format _____has an unpredictable format

is socially intimate_____is businesslike

is polite and agreeable _____is vocal and challenging

is accountable _____leaves each person
to one another   on their own

is mutually supportive _____has optional support

includes social events _____exists for meetings only

is calm _____is chaotic

ministers to people _____focuses on our
outside the group   own business

allows difficult questions _____is more focused on
                                                                                            unity and consensus

has strong leadership _____is group-led

results in long-term _____relationships end
relationships   when meetings do

actively recruits new members _____is closed to new members

State of Mind

What is your state of mind? Are you frazzled? Thrilled? Confused? Based on your "state of mind," you need to choose a "state flag," a "state bird," a "state song" and a "state flower." Complete the various statements below and take turns sharing your answers with your group.

My "state of mind" could be called:_____

My "state bird" is (peacock, cuckoo, goose, etc.):_____

My "state flower" is a (snapdragon, sunflower, pansy, etc.):_____

My "state song" is:_____

My "state flag" looks like:

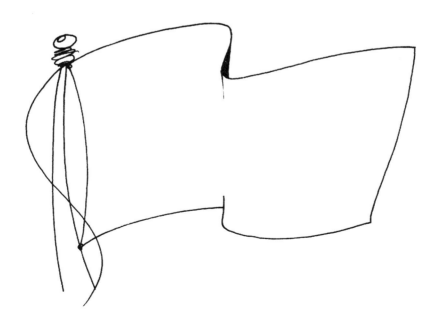

Self-Scale

Help your group get to know you better. Use the following word-pairs to select the description that fits you the best. Take turns sharing your answers.

Impulsive _____Cautious

Relaxed _____Tense

Self-confident _____Unsure

Modest _____Boastful

Mature _____Childish

Childlike _____Stuffy

Agreeable _____Disagreeable

Spontaneous _____Predictable

Close_____Distant

Friendly _____Aloof

Compassionate_____Apathetic

Kind _____Self-focused

Compulsive _____Flexible

Industrious _____Lazy

Straight-forward _____Indirect

Ambitious _____Complacent

Competitive_____Noncompetitive

Generous _____Stingy

Happy _____Sad

Whispers

This is a fun game similar to "Telephone" or "Rumors" and it can help everyone get better acquainted. "Whispers" can also be used as a lesson on communication skills and gossip.

The game begins with one person choosing one of the questions listed below and thinking of a three to five word sentence answer. Then that person whispers their answer to the person on their right. The person on their right whispers the message to the person to their right, and so on. After the message goes around the circle, the last person tells the group what they heard. This "whispered version" is then compared to the original story.

1. "My most embarrassing moment ..."

2. "One time when nature couldn't wait ..."

3. "My funniest experience on a date ..."

4. "The worst meal I ever had ..."

5. "One time I got stopped by the police ..."

6. "The best vacation I ever had ..."

7. "A practical joke I tried once ..."

8. "Once, when I was at summer camp ..."

9. "The best birthday party I ever had ..."

Family Classics

We all have great family memories of hilarious episodes which have become "family classics." These are the stories that someone is sure to tell every time the family is together. Help your group get to know you and your family a little better by sharing one or two of the following fun family memories.

1. A funny thing that happened one Christmas ...

2. A funny thing that happened on vacation ...

3. A funny thing that happened at the dinner table ...

4. A funny thing that happened that mom and dad never knew about ...

5. A funny thing that happened at a family outing ...

6. A funny thing a brother or sister would prefer to have left unsaid ...

7. A funny thing that happened at a family reunion ...

8. A funny thing that happened at grandma and grandpa's ...

9. A funny story that mom and dad would rather forget ...

10. A funny thing that embarrassed the whole family in front of many people ...

11. A funny family memory about me ...

My ABC's

You have many interesting qualities and your group would like to know about them! How about 26 ways to describe yourself? Using the entire alphabet or the letters of your name, choose words that describe yourself. You even have some examples! Then go around the group and take turns sharing your answers.

A is for_____ (active, adventurous, affirming, accountable ...)

B is for_____ (bashful, busy, bored, beautiful, bodacious ...)

C is for_____ (cautious, calm, courageous, conventional ...)

D is for_____ (daring, defiant, devoted, desperate, dizzy ...)

E is for_____ (elegant, enthusiastic, effervescent, envious ...)

F is for_____ (fun, futuristic, food-loving, fast, ferocious ...)

G is for_____ (giddy, gracious, gentle, growing, genuine ...)

H is for_____ (happy, hopeful, hectic, hot-tempered, hip ...)

I is for_____ (inventive, intelligent, industrious, ingenious ...)

J is for _____ (jolly, joyful, jazzy, junk-loving, jumpy ...)

K is for_____ (knowledgeable, keen, keyed-up, kind, kinetic ...)

L is for_____ (loyal, lonely, lovable, loving, lighthearted ...)

M is for_____ (mischievous, mad, musical, mall-loving ...)

N is for_____ (normal, nifty, nocturnal, nappy, nurturing ...)

O is for_____ (optimistic, open, outspoken, odd, opulent ...)

P is for_____ (persistent, passionate, peaceful, patient ...)

Q is for_____ (quiet, quick, quizzical, quintessential ...)

R is for_____ (rambunctious, romantic, real, reflective ...)

S is for_____ (sad, spiritual, super-duper, shy, sensitive ...)

T is for_____ (tall, tough, tender, trendy, tacky, thoughtful ...)

U is for_____ (unstoppable, uunhinged, upbeat, uptight ...)

V is for_____ (visionary, vulnerable, vibrant, vintage ...)

W is for_____ (warm, whimsical, wise, weary, worried ...)

X is for_____ (xylophonist, x-ray vision, xenophobic, x-citing ...)

Y is for_____ (young-at-heart, yuppie, yackety, yielding ...)

Z is for_____ (zany, zealous, zestful, zoned-out, zonked ...)

Famous Firsts

Unlock your memory box and share a little bit of your personal history. Choose two or three of the "firsts" listed below and take turns sharing your answers.

The first time I kissed someone ...

The first time I went on a real date ...

The first time I attended a formal event ...

The first time I remember my mom or dad ...

The first time I tried to swim or jump off a diving board ...

The first time I gave someone a present ...

The first time I drove a car ...

The first time I got a traffic ticket ...

The first time I was in a schoolyard scuffle ...

The first time I smoked a cigarette ...

The first time I threw up in public ...

The first time I went to school ...

The first time I hurt myself playing ...

The first time I cooked something ...

Toy Box

Each of us has a history. Learning more about one another's backgrounds can help a group understand and appreciate each other even more. Use the questions below to help you discuss your childhood and your childhood toys.

1. What were your favorite toys when you were a child?

2. Which ones do you still have?

3. What games did you play at recess and with the kids in the neighborhood?

4. What was your favorite birthday or Christmas present when you were in grade school?

5. What board games and other games did you play with your family?

6. What did you do when you had a friend over to spend the night?

7. What was the one toy you always wanted and never got?

Spiritual Inventory

Answer the following questions to give your group an idea of your spiritual life. Feel free to come up with your own answers other than the ones listed.

1. Lately, my prayers remind me of ...
   - ❏ helium balloons—I pray about something and let it go.
   - ❏ wet fireworks—My prayers seem like duds.
   - ❏ shopping carts—Basically, I've been asking God for stuff.
   - ❏ broken records—I keep praying the same thing over and over.
   - ❏ rubber ceilings—My prayers seem to bounce right back.
   - ❏ Robinson Crusoe's Island—I feel all alone, like no one's there.
   - ❏ telephone calls—Answers seem to come quickly and clearly.
   - ❏ other:_____

2. My church involvement could best be described as a/an ...
   - ❏ yo-yo—Let's just say that I'm not real consistent.
   - ❏ five-course dinner—It's been extremely satisfying for me.
   - ❏ blue horse—To tell the truth, it's more nonexistent.
   - ❏ dog on a leash—I only go if I'm dragged.
   - ❏ bench warmer—I'm on the team and ready to play, but haven't been asked.
   - ❏ bandwagon—I'm ready to go if there's a crowd.
   - ❏ heart surgery—It's been lifechanging!
   - ❏ eager beaver—I look forward to a bunch of different church events.
   - ❏ other:_____

3. My attempts to live as an example of Jesus are most like ...
   - ❏ a mirror—I have offered others a good reflection of Christ's love.
   - ❏ Dr. Jekyll and Mr. Hyde—I have my good moments and my not-so-good moments.
   - ❏ The Invisible Man—I guess I'm too busy to think about living like someone else.
   - ❏ a microscope—Well, if you look close enough you can see Jesus.
   - ❏ a telescope—Well, if you look from a distance I'm a pretty good example.
   - ❏ a full moon—I'm a good example about once a month.
   - ❏ other:_____

The "One Anothers"

The Bible lists many different "one anothers," describing how church members should relate to each other. A Christian group is a great place for these "one anothers" to happen. Which "one another" do you need right now? Share your choice with the group.

DEVOTION AND HONOR: *Be devoted to one another in brotherly love. Honor one another above yourselves.*   Romans 12:10

ACCEPTANCE: *Accept one another, then, just as Christ accepted you, in order to bring praise to God.*   Romans 15:7

SERVICE: *You, my brothers, were called to be free. But do not use your freedom to indulge the sinful nature; rather, serve one another in love.*   Galatians 5:13

KINDNESS, COMPASSION OR FORGIVENESS: *Be kind and compassionate to one another, forgiving each other, just as in Christ God forgave you.*
Ephesians 4:32

ENCOURAGEMENT: *Therefore encourage one another and build each other up, just as in fact you are doing.*   1 Thessalonians 5:11

HOSPITALITY: *Offer hospitality to one another without grumbling.*   1 Peter 4:9

HARMONY: *Finally, all of you, live in harmony with one another; be sympathetic, love as brothers, be compassionate and humble.*   1 Peter 3:8

INSTRUCTION: *I myself am convinced, my brothers, that you yourselves are full of goodness, complete in knowledge and competent to instruct one another.*
Romans 15:14

MOTIVATING: *And let us consider how we may spur one another on toward love and good deeds.*   Hebrews 10:24

CARE: *... so that there should be no division in the body, but that its parts should have equal concern for each other.*   1 Corinthians 12:25

PEACE: *"Salt is good, but if it loses its saltiness, how can you make it salty again? Have salt in yourselves, and be at peace with each other."*   Mark 9:50

BUILDING UP: *Therefore encourage one another and build each other up, just as in fact you are doing.*   1 Thessalonians 5:11

Time Will Tell

We all seem so busy. If only we had a little more time! How do you feel about time? Do you have enough time? Do you feel rushed? Are you bored? Which one of the images below best describes your feelings about time? Choose the one which fits you and share your answers with the group. Your group might choose to try and guess each other's answers ...

Cuckoo Clock
My schedule drives me crazy! You should see my daily calendar!

Indigo
I keep such late hours my timepiece has to glow in the dark.

VCR Clock
I can't seem to figure out this time thing. I need help!

Stopwatch
My life seems like a race against the clock. Faster! Faster!!

Big Ben
Getting places on time is central to my life. I'm always hearing alarm buzzes and bells.

Hour Glass
My schedule is very structured. My time is measured in tiny pieces.

Sundial
I'm not into schedules. Looking at the sun is close enough for me.

Pocket Watch
My attitude toward time is old-fashioned, early to bed and early to rise.

Annoying Alarm Clock
Clocks and I don't get along very well. They make me grumpy.

Toy Clock
My kids are my clock. I plan my day according to their schedule.

Dashboard Clock
I spend so much time on the road that I drive in my sleep.

Wind-up Clock
I'm so busy I have to be careful I don't wind down!

Romans Inventory

This is an activity adapted from *The Serendipity Encyclopedia* (available from Serendipity, 1-800-525-9563). It is a survey based on Romans 12:9–21. The passage is about how church members should relate to one another. Read the passage out loud, answer the questions below and then take turns sharing your results.

LOVE MUST BE SINCERE: I am able to really give myself to others, not in some phony way, but with real meaning.

     1   2   3   4   5   6   7   8   9   10

HATE WHAT IS EVIL; CLING TO WHAT IS GOOD: I am learning to stand up for my convictions; to say no to something I know is wrong and yes to God.

     1   2   3   4   5   6   7   8   9   10

BE DEVOTED TO ONE ANOTHER IN BROTHERLY LOVE. HONOR ONE ANOTHER ABOVE YOURSELVES. I am learnng how to reach out and hug my Christian brothers and sisters—for the right reasons. And I put their needs above my own.

     1   2   3   4   5   6   7   8   9   10

KEEP YOUR SPIRITUAL FERVOR, SERVING THE LORD: I am eager and enthusiastic to do anything I can for Christ because my heart is full of gratitude for what he has done for me.

     1   2   3   4   5   6   7   8   9   10

PATIENT IN AFFLICTION: Problems don't always get me down. I can take the heat. Under pressure I can stay cool.

     1   2   3   4   5   6   7   8   9   10

SHARE WITH GOD'S PEOPLE WHO ARE IN NEED. PRACTICE HOSPITALITY. I have learned that my possession, my time, my whole being belongs to God—to be shared with those in need.

     1   2   3   4   5   6   7   8   9   10

BLESS THOSE WHO PERSECUTE YOU. I have learned to respond with kindness to those wh o put me down—and to pray on their behalf. I am no longer defensive about my life.

     1   2   3   4   5   6   7   8   9   10

REJOICE WITH THOSE WHO REJOICE; MOURN WITH THOSE WHO MOURN. I celebrate life when others are rejoicing, and grieve openly when others are hurting. I am not afraid to show my feelings.

     1   2   3   4   5   6   7   8   9   10

Face the Facts

Use your artistic skills to tell your group how things are going. Answer the questions by using the outlines to draw your facial expressions. If you felt great yesterday, draw a happy-looking version of your face. If you woke up this morning feeling grumpy with bad hair, draw how you felt. Take turns telling your group how you are feeling by showing one another the faces you have drawn.

Last night, when I reflected on my day, I felt ...

When I woke up this morning, I felt ...

By the middle of the day today, I felt ...

Right before I came to this meeting, I felt ...

When I look ahead to tomorrow, I feel ...

Groovy Grandparents

In the old days, extended families spent more time together and lived in the same town and city. Today, families have become more separated. Many of us have not spent the time with our grandparents that we would have liked. Take turns sharing your answers to the following questions. If you did not know your grandparents, perhaps you know stories about them, or you knew their brothers and sisters.

1. What are some physical characteristics and personality traits you got from your grandparents?

2. How would people from your grandparents' town describe them?

3. What are your fondest memories of your grandparents?

4. What qualities did your grandparents have that you would like to have in your life?

5. How have your grandparents treated you in ways that no one else can?

6. Introduce one of your grandparents to the group by telling a story about them.

The Tortoise and the Hare

How fast have you been going lately? What pace has your life been moving at recently? Choose one of the items below (or think up your own) which reminds you of the pace of your life and then take turns sharing your answers with the group.

Battery-powered Bunny
I just keep going and going. I wonder when I am ever going to stop!

Space Shuttle
I blast off brightly, get my work done, and then coast back to earth ready to blast off again.

Stately Riverboat
I take it easy. I paddle along elegantly down a gently flowing river.

Scooter
I may not set any speed records, but I putt-putt along and go where I need to go.

Conked-out Convertible
I'm happy to sit in the sun and not go anywhere. I already have enough miles on me.

Farm Tractor
I work hard and pull big loads. I don't move fast but I move mountains.

Formula 1 Race Car
I am the fastest one around, but I need a lot of attention when I pull in the pits.

Roller Coaster
My pace changes drastically. My pattern is slowly up, up, up and then go super-fast.

Overworked Airlines
I get a tight schedule, make numerous "flights" a day and am ready for the hangar every night.

49

Relax!

Are you under a lot of stress? How do you relax when you begin to feel run-down or anxious? Take a moment to answer the questions below and then take turns sharing your answers with your group.

1. The best way to get me tense or upset is to:
   - ❑ make me late for something
   - ❑ make me navigate a bureaucracy
   - ❑ be betrayed by friends or coworkers
   - ❑ take me for granted
   - ❑ overdraw my checking account
   - ❑ hide something I need
   - ❑ put me in a line or traffic
   - ❑ give me too much work
   - ❑ get in trouble at school
   - ❑ other:_____

2. When I get tense, tired or upset, my first response is to :
   - ❑ become angry
   - ❑ bite my nails
   - ❑ drive fast
   - ❑ get tense shoulders
   - ❑ go shopping
   - ❑ get drunk
   - ❑ eat, eat, eat
   - ❑ withdraw
   - ❑ feel sick
   - ❑ mistreat others
   - ❑ cry
   - ❑ smoke
   - ❑ panic
   - ❑ get impatient
   - ❑ other:_____

3. One thing that helps me relax is to:
   - ❑ listen to music
   - ❑ talk to a friend
   - ❑ get a massage
   - ❑ work in the yard
   - ❑ read a helpful book
   - ❑ buy myself flowers
   - ❑ take a walk
   - ❑ make a list
   - ❑ play with a little kid
   - ❑ write it in my journal
   - ❑ pray
   - ❑ play with my pet
   - ❑ work out
   - ❑ do a hobby:_____
   - ❑ other:_____

4. This week, to relax I am going to:

   Signature_____

How Do I Love Thee?

This is an activity adapted from *The Serendipity Encyclopedia* (available from Serendipity, 1-800-525-9563). It is a survey based on part of 1 Corinthians 13, also known as the "Love Chapter." This activity will help you learn more about how well you love others. Read the passage aloud, answer the questions below and take turns sharing your answers with your group.

LOVE IS PATIENT: I don't take out my frustrations on those I love. I am calm under pressure and careful with my tongue.

1	2	3	4	5	6	7	8	9	10

LOVE IS KIND: I go out of my way to say nice words and do thoughtful things for others.

1	2	3	4	5	6	7	8	9	10

LOVE DOES NOT ENVY: I am not envious of others' gifts and abilities or of what they have. Neither am I jealous with my time toward those who need me.

1	2	3	4	5	6	7	8	9	10

LOVE DOES NOT BOAST: I don't consider my role any more important than those I love—or talk like "I know better."

1	2	3	4	5	6	7	8	9	10

LOVE IS NOT RUDE: I don't make cutting or crude remarks when I don't get my way—or become silent and withdrawn.

1	2	3	4	5	6	7	8	9	10

LOVE IS NOT SELF-SEEKING: I don't put myself first. I try to give those I love spiritual and emotional support.

1	2	3	4	5	6	7	8	9	10

LOVE IS NOT EASILY ANGERED: I don't let little things bother me, especially with those I love. I have a muffler on my mouth.

1	2	3	4	5	6	7	8	9	10

LOVE KEEPS NO RECORD OF WRONGS: I don't keep score of the number of times those I love have said something or done something that upset me, and I don't bring it up when we have conflict.

1	2	3	4	5	6	7	8	9	10

My Job Is Like ...

How's your job going? Whether you work at home, for a corporation or for yourself, how would you describe your job? Choose one of the descriptions below which best describes your job and take turns sharing your answers with the group.

Uphill Battle
I'm always behind and keep getting behinder!

Frankenstein's Laboratory
My job is vibrant and creative.

Pressure Cooker
The stress is driving me nuts!

Newly Frozen Pond
I'm always on edge because I feel like I'm skating on thin ice.

Drying Paint
My job is so boring and monotonous that it's like watching paint dry.

100-yard dash
I get tired of always competing with my coworkers.

Gossip Factory
If everyone stopped gossiping, we'd get some work done!

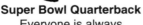

Piece of Cake
My job is so easy I could do it blindfolded.

Amusement Park
I almost feel guilty because my job is so much fun.

National Monument
I feel great about my job because what I do is important and meaningful!

Super Bowl Quarterback
Everyone is always depending on me to make all the right decisions.

Air-conditioned Igloo
Most of the time my job seems absolutely pointless.

My School Is Like ...

Tell the group what it's like at your school. Choose one of the descriptions below which best describes your experience at your school and take turns sharing your answers with the group. For group members who are not in school, use "My Job Is Like ..." on page 52.

A Fox Hunt
Everyone enjoys selecting one person to single out.

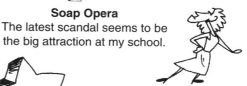

Soap Opera
The latest scandal seems to be the big attraction at my school.

A Fashion Show
More attention is given to what people wear than who they really are.

ESPN Convention
Our school revolves around the latest sport and the latest star athlete.

CIA
Everyone at my school is always trying to see what they can get away with.

The Emerald City
My school is a place where your dreams can come true.

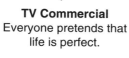

TV Commercial
Everyone pretends that life is perfect.

Chess Tournament
My school is always challenging me to solve problems.

A Learning Factory
My school is a great place to learn all kinds of wonderful things.

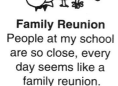

The Civil War
Everything gets disrupted by groups that can't get along.

Family Reunion
People at my school are so close, every day seems like a family reunion.

Chicken Coop
The main activity at my school is establishing a pecking order.

The Perfect Job

Sometimes describing an ideal situation can help us move toward it. What about your job? Many of us spend at least 40 hours a week at our jobs. When so much of our lives are spent at one thing, certainly we should consider ways to make it as great as possible. Imagine what your perfect job would be, fill in the spaces below and then take turns sharing your answers with the group.

1. The BUSINESS I would like to be in:

2. The COMPANY I would like to work for:

3. The POSITION I would like to have in this company:

4. The GEOGRAPHIC LOCATION I would like this job to be at:

5. The WORK SPACE I would enjoy the most:

6. The SCHEDULE I would like to keep:

7. The COMPENSATION I think I should get for this job:

8. The BENEFITS I would like to have:

9. I would like my COWORKERS to be:

10. What can you do to make your current job more like your perfect job?

 Pray that each person's job becomes more like their ideal job.

The Perfect School

Sometimes describing an ideal situation can help us move toward it. This also includes your school. Even though going to school is not always an option, there are plenty of ways we can make it better. Imagine what your perfect school would be, fill in the spaces below and take turns sharing your answers with the group. After everyone is finished, let each person share how they can make their school situation better.

1. The GEOGRAPHIC LOCATION where I would like to attend school is ...

2. The EXTRACURRICULAR ACTIVITIES I would really enjoy are ...

3. The LIVING CONDITIONS I would prefer are ...

4. The CAMPUS I would like to be on every day would be ...

5. The kind of PROFESSORS or TEACHERS I would like to have are ...

6. The COURSES I would like to take are ...

7. The DEGREE I would like to pursue is ...

8. The SOCIAL LIFE I would like to enjoy would be ...

9. The GRADUATION REQUIREMENTS I would like the most are ...

10. The CLASSMATES I would like to learn with would be ...

11. The SCHOOL I would like to attend is ...

 Pray that each person's school experience becomes more like their ideal school.

Great Bosses and Teachers

It's always a good idea to acknowledge those bosses and teachers we've known who had exceptional qualities. Recognizing great bosses and teachers helps us respect those people in roles of authority. In addition, when we have the opportunity to influence others as leaders we can strive for similar qualities.

Take turns sharing your answers to the following questions:

1. Who was the best boss or teacher you ever had? Why was this person so special?

2. What do you find most admirable about your current (or most recent) boss or one of your current (or most recent) teachers? Tell a story that illustrates this trait.

3. Which of the following characteristics are most important to you regarding your idea of a great boss or teacher? (Feel free to share characteristics not on this list.)

   ❒ encouraging   ❒ knowledgeable   ❒ friendly
   ❒ easy going   ❒ disciplined   ❒ clear
   ❒ trusting   ❒ inspirational   ❒ sincere
   ❒ polite   ❒ respectful   ❒ fair
   ❒ good reputation ❒ understanding   ❒ appreciative
   ❒ focused   ❒ interesting   ❒ funny
   ❒ interested   ❒ available   ❒ other:_____

4. If you are, or ever become, someone's boss or teacher, what strengths can you bring to the position?

I Am Like This Object ...

Choose an object in the room which you can use to describe yourself. You might choose a lamp because you enjoy illuminating the truth, you might choose an electrical outlet because you like to empower people, or you might choose the coffee maker because you like to wake people up. Take turns going around the group explaining what you have chosen and why.

Great Employees and Students

What makes a great employee or student? Take turns answering the following questions and sharing your answers with the group.

1. What was your favorite job or class?

2. What was the worst job or class you ever experienced?

3. What was the best student or coworker you ever knew? What made that person so good at what they do?

4. If you were teaching someone or hiring someone, what five qualities would you look for?

openness	eagerness	enthusiasm
sense of humor	team spirit	loyalty
perseverance	intelligence	curiosity
motivation	self-starter	unorthodox
cooperation	quiet	argumentative
skeptical	accepting	passive
aggressive	workaholic	creative

5. As a student or an employee, what are your greatest strengths and weaknesses?

It's Not Bragging!

How would you like to do some boasting ... about yourself? Saying good things about yourself and things you have done is a positive thing to do. Choose several of the questions below and share your answers with the group. Remember, it's not bragging if it's true and if someone asked you to talk about it.

1. What is your greatest accomplishment?

2. What are your best qualities at work?

3. What is something you can do that no one in your group can do?

4. What subject did you do best in at school?

5. What is the best thing you have done to support a nonprofit organization?

6. What is the nicest thing you have ever done for a neighbor?

7. What is the best gift you ever gave someone?

8. What is the best thing you ever did for someone younger than yourself?

9. What are your best qualities in a close relationship?

10. What is the kindest thing you have ever done for a stranger?

11. What is the best job you've ever done on an at-home project?

12. What is the nicest thing you have ever done for someone less fortunate than yourself?

Cartoons

Take a look at the different cartoons. How would you feel in the different situations? Write in your thoughts or comments in each cartoon and then share your answers with the group.

Bizarre Questions

Here are some strange questions you don't hear every day. These questions will help your group understand you better as you try to think up new ways to express yourself. Choose several of the questions below and take turns sharing your answers with the group:

1. What color is your favorite song?

2. What does your family life smell like?

3. What does your current mood look like?

4. What does your physical health sound like?

5. What is the melody of your job or school satisfaction?

6. What does your job taste like?

7. Describe the texture of your life dream.

8. What noise or sound would you use to describe your spiritual life?

9. What flavor is your favorite work of art?

10. What color is your romantic life?

Be-Attitudes

This is an activity adapted from *The Serendipity Encyclopedia* (available from Serendipity, 1-800-525-9563). This is a questionnaire based on Matthew 5:3–10, also known as the Beatitudes. Read the Scripture passage aloud, answer the questions below and then take turns sharing your answers with the group.

POOR IN SPIRIT: I can feel accepted by God when I feel most unacceptable to myself. I am a person of worth and value even though I don't have it all together.

   1   2   3   4   5   6   7   8   9   10

MOURN: I can show my feelings and let others know when I'm hurting. I can be around others when they are hurting without feeling embarrassment. I can weep like Jesus did.

   1   2   3   4   5   6   7   8   9   10

MEEK: I don't have to act like a hero or look like a beauty queen. I can just be myself—the person God made me.

   1   2   3   4   5   6   7   8   9   10

SPIRITUAL HUNGER: I am more excited about God's will for my life than my own success, popularity or good time. I am excited about knowing God.

   1   2   3   4   5   6   7   8   9   10

MERCIFUL: I can feel the pain of someone who is hurting, and care for them as God's representative. I really hurt when my friends hurt.

   1   2   3   4   5   6   7   8   9   10

PURE IN HEART: I can be open and honest with God and others. I don't have to put on a false mask or pretend to be something that I am not.

   1   2   3   4   5   6   7   8   9   10

PEACEMAKER: I work at keeping communication channels open and resolving conflicts—particularly with my family and friends who I love the most.

   1   2   3   4   5   6   7   8   9   10

PERSECUTION: I can take criticism without reacting defensively or feeling self-pity. I can take the heat and stand alone if I have to.

   1   2   3   4   5   6   7   8   9   10

Healthy Goals

How healthy are you? What do you do to stay healthy? What do you need to do to become healthier? Our health is important because it directly affects the quality of our lives and our ability to serve God. This Jump Start can be very helpful because you can discuss health-related goals and even hold one another accountable if your group chooses to do so. Answer the following questions and take turns sharing your answers. Then share ways to become healthier.

1. During the last 24 hours, I consumed the following:

	Vege-tables	Fruits	Meat	Bread / Grains	Dairy Products	Water	Junk Food
Number of Servings							

2. My sleep habits during the past week could best be described as:
   ❏ restful—I woke up refreshed and ready to go.
   ❏ adequate—My sleep was good enough to get me by.
   ❏ insufficient—I didn't sleep well or sleep enough.

3. My exercise habits during the past month could best be described as ...
   ❏ tremendous—I worked out four or more times each week.
   ❏ pretty good—I worked out two or three times a week.
   ❏ okay—I worked out once or twice a week last month.
   ❏ lousy—I hardly exercised at all last month.

4. On a scale of 0 to 10, my stress level lately has been:

0	5	10
I'm so tense I'm spitting battery acid.		I'm so relaxed people call me Raggedy Ann/Andy.

5. Recently, I've been known to partake in:
   ❏ caffeinated drinks   ❏ tobacco products
   ❏ other products I should probably avoid   ❏ alcoholic beverages

6. To be more healthy, I need to:

Ups and Downs at Work and School

Has your job or career been a good experience for you? Use the graph below to chart the ups and downs of your work life. You can plot your current job or your entire working career, beginning with your first lemonade stand. Ups might be raises, promotions or the beginning of an exciting new job. Downs might be a lousy boss, scheming coworkers, or low pay. After you fill in your chart, take turns telling the group about your ups and downs at work.

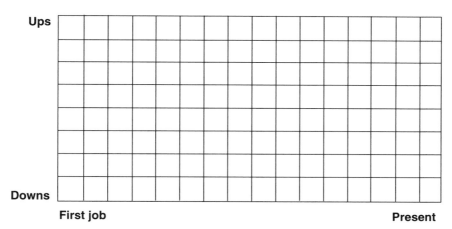

Ups

Downs

First job   **Present**

Use the graph below to chart the ups and downs of your educational life. Begin with nursery school or kindergarten and plot your high points and low points all the way to your last class. Ups and downs might include graduation, difficult semesters, lousy classes and fulfilling personal achievements. Take turns telling the group about your school experiences.

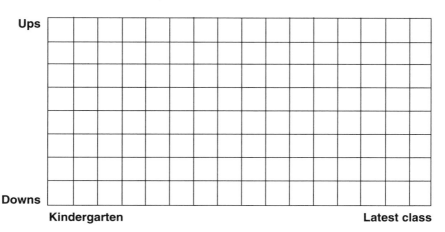

Ups

Downs

Kindergarten   **Latest class**

Personal Weather Station

How's the weather in your life today? Using the different gauges below, fill in the measurements on your personal weather station. Instead of the wind direction, what is your life direction? Instead of the temperature of the air, what is the temperature of your love life? What warnings or watches are in effect in your life right now?

After you fill in the data on your personal weather station, take turns telling the group about the weather in your life.

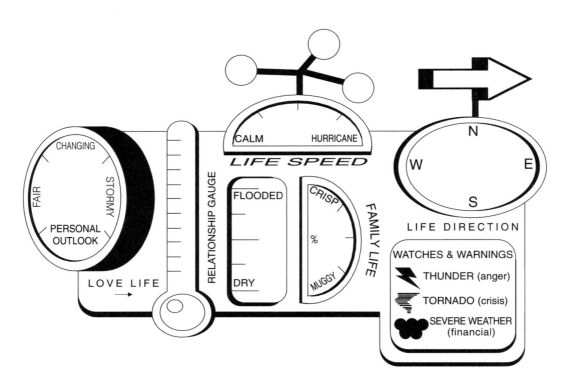

Spiritual Journey

Here are some questions that will help your group gain a better understanding of your spiritual journey. Take a few moments to complete the sentences and take turns sharing some of your responses with the group.

1. One of my earliest memories of church is ...

2. The first person I knew who seemed to live a life positively influenced by their religion was...

3. One of the first times I really felt like I needed God's help was ...

4. The first time I remembered hearing about Jesus was ...

5. The first time I considered personally accepting what Jesus accomplished for me was ...

6. Since my personal encounter with Jesus Christ, my Christian life could be best described as ...

7. Currently, my Christian life is ...

8. My church involvement could be described as ...

9. One thing I would like to see change in the way I follow Christ is ...

10. One way I see myself serving God in the future is ...

If I Knew I Could Not Fail ...

Sometimes the fear of failure keeps us from trying new things or striving for accomplishments. For this Jump Start, think of things you would like to do in your life *if you knew you could not fail.* Write down your answers in the space provided and then take turns sharing your answers with the group.

If I knew I could not fail, one thing I would like to do around the house is ...

If I knew I could not fail, one thing I would like to accomplish at work or at school is ...

If I knew I could not fail, one thing I would like to try in my social relationships is ...

If I knew I could not fail, one thing I would like to try regarding my personal improvement is ...

If I knew I could not fail, one thing I would like to do in my family relationships is ...

If I knew I could not fail, one daring, risky thing I've always wanted to do is ...

If I knew I could not fail, one thing I would like to do to serve God is ...

Friendship Rally

We all need friends. There are times in our lives when we especially need the support friends can provide. Here are some questions which will help you learn about your friendships and the friendships of your group members. Take a moment to answer the following questions and then take turns sharing your answers with the group.

1. When was the last time you found yourself surrounded by a group of your best friends?

2. When did you need help or support and your friends rallied around you?

3. When did you need the love and support of your friends but found yourself alone, needing your friends but struggling without them?

4. What can you do to make sure your friends are there when you need them?
   - ❏ ask them for help when I need it
   - ❏ get better friends
   - ❏ be there for them when they need a hand
   - ❏ be more open with my feelings
   - ❏ do a better job staying in touch
   - ❏ be more hospitable, giving and outgoing
   - ❏ other:_____

5. What can you do to be a better friend?

6. How can your friends help you today?

Relationships Wanted

Everyone needs relationships. As a matter of fact, we all need a variety of relationships to meet our various needs. Look over the list below and mark the relationships you need in your life. Take turns sharing your choices with the group.

☐ PLAYMATES: I need people to play with, so I can have fun and not lose my childlike qualities.

☐ MENTOR: I need someone to blaze a trail for me and stand by me when I need advice and encouragement.

☐ BIG BROTHER: I need someone who will protect me when I get threatened or when things get tough.

☐ CONFIDANT: I need someone who will listen carefully and let me say everything I need to say and keep my secrets.

☐ PRAYER PARTNER: I need someone I can pray with who is faithful and dependable—someone I can trust.

☐ PEERS: I need more people in my life who have the same values, lifestyle and goals that I have.

☐ FATHER FIGURE: I need someone who will be like a father to me—the way fathers are supposed to be.

☐ DEVIL'S ADVOCATE: I need someone in my life who will challenge me, including my choices and my beliefs.

☐ GRANDPARENTS: I need some older folks in my life so I can benefit from their wisdom and maturity.

☐ BIG SISTER: I need an older woman I can go to for encouragement, guidance and friendship.

☐ BUDDIES: I need friends who I can just hang out with and be myself.

☐ MOTHER FIGURE: I need a motherly person in my life who will love and nurture me and help me make important decisions.

☐ OTHER:_____

Read My Face

This is a fun Jump Start which will help your group get to know you better. The rules are simple. For each of the different areas of your life, you make a face that demonstrates how you are feeling about that subject. The group guesses how you are feeling based on the expression you have made. Each person takes turns sharing their facial expressions on the various topics.

1. How I feel about the day I had TODAY:

2. How I feel about my JOB or SCHOOL:

3. How I feel about my ROMANTIC relationship:

4. How I feel about my FAMILY:

5. How I feel about my SPIRITUAL LIFE:

6. How I feel about my FRIENDSHIPS:

7. How I feel about my FINANCIAL SITUATION:

8. How I feel about my HEALTH:

9. How I feel about my FUTURE:

Life Map

Where have you been during your life? Where have your life's adventures taken you? Using the map below, draw the path of your life journey. What places did you visit? Some locations have been included on this map ("Pinnacle Peak," "Sweltering Swamp," etc.), but feel free to add your own. What kind of roads did you use? When did you cross over into new life areas or stages? When did you face struggles or successes? Start in Birthtown and trace your life's journey all the way to Todaysville, then take turns sharing the highlights of your life journey with your group.

You're Fired!

It finally happened. Just when you got it figured out, your job has been replaced by a robot. Technology has run its course and whether you are a cab driver, an attorney or a homemaker, your job has been automated.

It's time to start looking for another job. What are you going to do? Take a moment to answer the following questions and then take turns sharing your responses with the group.

1. If you found out you could not do your current job, how would you feel?

2. What would it be like if you had to leave your job, the projects you are working on and your coworkers?

3. What would you do once you left your job?
   - ❐ take a vacation
   - ❐ stay in bed all day and feel sorry for myself
   - ❐ kick back for a few days and rest
   - ❐ do all the things I've been too busy to do
   - ❐ start immediately looking for another job
   - ❐ panic
   - ❐ other:_____

4. When you finally started looking for another job, what kind of job would you look for?

5. What kind of experiences have you had in the past when you have been job hunting?

6. What strategies would you use in your efforts to find another job?

7. How would you maintain your sanity and your sense of well-being while you looked for something else?

8. How would your faith in God help you as you looked for another job?

Funny Money

How would you describe your financial habits? Each of us deals with our money differently. Your group might benefit from a discussion about these issues. Look over the different descriptions below and choose the one that best describes your approach to money and finances. Then take turns sharing your answers with the group.

Pair of Dice
I enjoy the excitement of risky financial decisions.

Carrot On a Stick
I like to use money to get people to do what I want.

Microscope
I watch every penny. I know where all my money goes.

Tight-lipped Clam
No one's ever going to get their hands on my pearl, uh, money.

Under the Rug
I sweep money issues under the rug. Out of sight, out of mind!

8-Ball
I'm in so much debt that I feel like I'm hiding behind the eight ball.

Shop-a-holic
I think that the best use of my money is to buy things with it.

Bulls and Bears
I'm a stock market junkie. I like Wall Street more than my bank.

King Midas
Making money is my greatest passion, even if there's a cost.

Cashier
I control how the money is dispersed and spent at my house.

Leaky Bucket
No matter how much I try to save, it all seems to disappear.

Happy Hermit
I've found that I'm happier without money and all it brings.

Life Chart

It helps your group members get to know you better if they can get an overall picture of your life. Use the chart below to record the most important events in your life. Then take turns telling your group about those events.

Age	Major Accomplishments	Tragedies and Crises	Important Milestones
1–6			
7–12			
13–18			
19–25			
26–35			
36–45			
46–60			
60+			

 Be sure to pray for one another for any recent crises and tragedies. You can affirm one another for the strengths you noticed in each person's major accomplishments.

Open Your Present

Life is great, especially without regret or worry. Regret is unfinished business that keeps us focused on the past, and worry is anxiety about upcoming events that keep us occupied with the future. Both worry and regret keep us from enjoying the present. To help you "open your present," list the unfinished business or other regrets from your past, then list things you are worried about happening in the future. After everyone is finished, take turns sharing what you wrote with the group, but only what you are comfortable sharing.

List the regrets and other unfinished business from your past:

List the things you are worried about happening in the future:

 Pray for one another that you can give God your regrets and worries, knowing that he is capable of taking care of them.

Coping Skills

We all have things we have to do that we don't enjoy doing. What do you have to do that you don't want to do? What dreaded activities, projects, deadlines, responsibilities and appointments are on your calendar (confronting a coworker, cleaning house, going to the dentist, exercising, paying bills, etc.). What do you do to avoid these tasks? What are the consequences of procrastination? How do you cope with these tasks? What tips and strategies have you discovered to assure the successful completion of these tasks? Fill in the chart below and take turns sharing your answers with the group.

Tasks I have to do that I don't want to do	What happens when I avoid doing these things	Positive ways I found to get these tasks done

Take a moment to affirm one another for the ways you are able to handle difficult tasks. Also pray for one another as you face these tasks.

100 Days ...

Uh-oh. Your journeys to the exotic jungles of central Serenesia have left you feeling a bit funky. It seems you have become the unwilling host of a nasty microorganism. Your doctor gives you the bad news. You have 100 days left to live. Yikes!

Now what? What are you going to do? Imagine that you are faced with such an awful prognosis. Answer the questions below and take turns sharing your answers with the group.

What are some things you would like to do in the next 100 days?

Which relationships would you like to "patch up" or improve in the next 100 days?

How will you live your life differently in the next 100 days?

What kind of plans will you make regarding your funeral?

How would the prognosis affect your faith in God?

Take Me to Your Leader!

Sometimes, a group of people need to choose a leader for an activity or Bible study. Take turns answering one of the questions and then vote on the best answer. The winner gets to be the leader!

1. How many speeding tickets have you had in the last six months?

2. How many pets do you have and what are their names?

3. Who was born closest / farthest to this location?

4. Whose birthday is closest to today?

5. Who has celebrated the most momentous milestone in the last year?

6. *For kids:* Who had to stay after school or go to the principal's office the most times last semester?

7. Who was the youngest person to kiss a member of the opposite sex (besides a family member or relative)?

8. Who has the most interesting story about something that happened to you on vacation?

9. Who has the best story about how their parents met?

10. Who has had the worst job experience?

11. Who has had the most memorable holiday misadventure?

12. Who has had the most embarrassing moment?

13. Who has had the worst experience with bureaucracy?

Church Bingo

Here is an adaptation of that Serendipity classic, "Human Bingo" (*Ice-Breakers and Heart-Warmers*, p. 31). To play "Church Bingo," after the leader yells "Go!," find people in your group who have done the different things written in the boxes. Get those people to sign the appropriate square. The winner is the first person to complete a row—horizontally, vertically or diagonally—and yells "Bingo!" Remember, each person may only sign your bingo card one time.

sang a solo during a worship service	parked in a visitor place	bought lunch for pastor this year	slept during church last week	regularly teaches Sunday school	knows names of all 12 apostles
knows all the books of the Bible	serves on a church committee	is an usher	is a member of the choir	has gone on a church retreat	is a charter member of the church
plays in church orchestra	knows names of the 12 tribes of Israel	leads a small group	works in the church nursery or day care	has perfect attendance in past six months	name was in last week's bulletin
recently put coins in collection plate	made an announce-ment at church recently	sits in the same pew every week	switched from another denomina-tion	has name imprinted on Bible	wearing Christian jewelry
can recite three Bible verses from memory	got married in a park	walks to church on Sunday	chaper-oned a youth retreat	doodles on bulletin during church	argues in Sunday school
can imper-sonate the pastor	has shared spiritual journey with con-gregation	helps maintain church facilities	hosts church group in home	can tell you their three favorite hymns	is on the church staff

If Today Was A ...

What kind of day have you had today? How would you describe it? Use the analogies below to tell your group about your day. Be creative!

IF TODAY WAS A FISH ...
- ❏ I'd throw it back
- ❏ it'd be a smelly ol' Carp
- ❏ I'd have it stuffed and mounted
- ❏ it'd be the big one that got away
- ❏ it'd be a beautiful 10-pound bass
- ❏ other:_____

IF TODAY WAS A MOVIE ...
- ❏ it'd be a tragedy
- ❏ it'd be a comedy
- ❏ it'd be a dubbed, out-of-sync foreign film
- ❏ I'd want to see it again and again
- ❏ I'd ask the theater manager for my money back
- ❏ other:_____

IF TODAY WAS A FOLK HERO ...
- ❏ it'd be John Henry who beat that steam drill
- ❏ it'd be Rip Van Winkle—ZZZZZZ!
- ❏ it'd be the Ghost of Sleepy Hollow—I lost my head!
- ❏ it'd be Paul Bunyan, larger than life!
- ❏ it'd be Johnny Appleseed—very fruitful
- ❏ other:_____

IF TODAY WAS A POLITICAL EVENT ...
- ❏ it'd be a rip-roaring debate
- ❏ it'd be a festive convention
- ❏ it'd be as important and solemn as an inauguration
- ❏ it'd be like a nail-biting election
- ❏ it'd be shaking babies and kissing hands
- ❏ other:_____

IF TODAY WAS A PLANET ...
- ❏ it'd be Mercury, too hot to handle
- ❏ it'd be Venus—love is in the air!
- ❏ it'd be Mars, because it was warlike
- ❏ it'd be Saturn, I ran rings and around everyone
- ❏ it'd be Pluto, cold and lonely
- ❏ other:_____

Knots

This is a fun way to get a group "jump-started" or to close a meeting. This activity is a great way to demonstrate how interconnected a group of people can be.

To play "Knots" have everyone stand in a circle, and grab two hands from any two people in the group. After everyone has two hands, the group works together to untangle their knot. One option is to try to untie the knot with everyone blindfolded! (Note: "Knots" is almost impossible with more than 20 people.)

Who Am I?

This is a super Jump Start for a large group. Prepare by writing names on the same number of cards as there are people in your group. These could be names of historical figures, local celebrities, athletes, literary characters or any well-known figure. Then tape these cards on everyone's back. When the leader says "Go!" everyone tries to figure out whose name is on their back by asking everyone else YES or NO questions. The first person to guess who they are is the winner.

After you have a winner, you can sort the group into smaller groups by organizing them according to categories: athletes, politicians, entertainers, literary characters, religious figures, commercial characters, children's characters, etc.

Curious George	Abraham Lincoln	Little Bo Peep
The Grinch	Cher	King Midas
Clarence Thomas	Spiderman	Pinocchio
Wilma Flintstone	Chef Boy-ar-dee	Minnie Mouse
Astro Jetson	Mrs. Butterworth	Dick Clark
Knute Rockne	Samuel Adams	Geraldine Ferraro
Amelia Earhart	Philemon	Robin Hood
Zeus	Mario Andretti	Kristie McAuliffe
Hillary Clinton	Mussolini	Spock
Olive Oyl	PeeWee Herman	Kareem Abdul-Jabbar
Kruschev	Tchaikovsky	Mario Cuomo
Winnie Mandela	Tiger Woods	Huey Long
Christopher Robin	Albert Schweitzer	Pythagoras
Jane Eyre	George Plimpton	Rumplestiltskin
Magellan	Godzilla	Cupid
Madame Curie	Coco Chanel	Pancho Villa
Michelangelo	Andy Warhol	Frank Lloyd Wright
Tom Selleck	Crocodile Dundee	Gloria Steinem
Quinn the Eskimo	Babar	Zorro
Oscar Meyer	Jonas Salk	Dennis the Menace
Ronald McDonald	Samuel Morse	Paul Revere
Galileo	Admiral Byrd	Faberge
Elvis Presley	Orville Redenbacher	Elizabeth Taylor
Paul Bunyan	The Great Pumpkin	Snow White
Porky Pig	Thor	Boy George
Jack Frost	Cleopatra	Marcus Welby, M.D.
Aristotle Onassis	Mike Ditka	Joe Montana
Mona Lisa	Dick Cavett	Mr. Clean
Barbie	The musical artist for-	George Bush
Arthur Ashe	merly known as Prince	Scooby Doo
Jules Verne	Zsa Zsa Gabor	Old McDonald

How to Form a Group

Anytime you have a large group of people, forming smaller groups quickly is important ... and fun! Use the following ideas and questions to create smaller groups out of larger ones.

1. Name tags can be a good way to form smaller groups. Use different color name tags and then group the blues, greens, etc. Further divide groups with different symbols, such as smiley faces and stars.

2. Group people by the season of the year they were born in (spring, summer, fall and winter).

3. Group people by where they would like to go on their next vacation: the mountains, the beach or the city.

4. Group people by the time zone they were born in (Eastern, Central, Mountain, Pacific and Other).

5. Use the following choices to split groups in half, fourths, eighths, etc.

   "Would you rather _____ or _____?"

read a book	play cards
make your bed	leave it messy
go to the opera	go bowling
ask for directions	keep looking
do yard work	do laundry
go on a blind date	go out with friends
wash the car	wash the dog
eat sushi	clean the toilet

6. Divide people by the kind of shoes they are wearing: with laces or without laces.

7. Group people by their favorite type of music: Gospel, Jazz, Country, Rock, Pop or Classical.

8. Pass out playing cards and ask everyone to form straights, flushes and full houses to form groups.

Sharing Questions

Here are 20 questions you can use to get a group talking. Sharing questions are great when you do not have much time. Read a question and let each group member share their answer, or let each person choose their own question. Generally, the questions are in order of the disclosure they require, from less disclosure to more disclosure. More sharing questions can be found on page 87.

1. What is your favorite book, movie and song?

2. What is your full name? What is your nickname? Where did you get your nickname? If you could pick a new name for yourself, what would it be?

3. If you could invent a machine to do one task you hate, what would you invent?

4. What is the greatest gift you ever received?

5. If you could live at any time in history what time would you choose?

6. You are hosting a dinner party and get to invite four famous people from history. Who are you going to invite?

7. If you could have any building in the world as your home, what would you choose?

8. Hollywood is making a moving about your incredible life! What actor or actress do you want to play you?

9. What event in history would you like to observe firsthand?

10. You got a package in the mail! What do you hope it contains? Who sent it?

11. If you could be present at any biblical event, what would you choose?

12. If you were designing your family crest, what four images would you put on it and why?

13. A banquet is held in your honor! What food would you like to have served?

14. If you could receive any award, which one would you like to receive? What did you do to deserve it?

15. What day in your life would you like to live over again? What year?

16. What three life lessons would you like to pass on to your children and grandchildren?

17. What is your greatest virtue?

18. Name one thing you wish you were taught as a child.

19. What three things would you like to change about your childhood?

20. What would you like to have written on your tombstone? Mentioned in your obituary? Who do you want to be your pallbearers?

Activity Bingo

This is a great Jump Start to get everyone revved up and having fun. After the leader says "Go!," find people in your group who can DO the different things listed in the boxes. After they demonstrate their skill, get them to sign the appropriate square. The winner is the first person to complete a row—horizontally, vertically or diagonally—and yells "Bingo!" Remember, each person may only sign your bingo card one time.

trumpet like an elephant	crow, peck and walk like a chicken	lie on the ground and fry like bacon	balance a coin on their nose for 10 seconds	yodel loudly	tell their most embarrass-ing moment
stand on their head	touch nose with tongue	pantomime riding a bucking bronco	quickly recite a tongue twister three times	whistle a tune you choose	yell like Tarzan so everyone can hear you
pirouette like a ballerina	talk like Donald Duck	imitate a Sumo wrestler	do a bird call	recite a limerick	do a cartwheel
juggle three items	do a somersault	tell a knock-knock joke	act like a mosquito	win three times at "rock, paper, scissors"	burp at will
cross their eyes	hop on one foot for 30 seconds	touch the ceiling	pop their knuckles	recite a nursery rhyme in pig Latin	zoom around the room like an airplane
dance the Charleston	do five push-ups	try to do the splits	tell a riddle	wiggle their ears	imitate a belly dancer

Even More Sharing Questions

Here are 20 more questions to get a group warmed up. Read a question and let each group member share their answer, or let each person choose their own question. Generally, the questions are in order of the disclosure they require, from less disclosure to more disclosure.

1. If you could have any pet, what would it be? Why?

2. What natural phenomena would you like to observe?

3. If you could walk into a dealership and buy any car, what would you choose? What options would you want? What personalized license plate would you request?

4. If you could have any job in the world, whose job would you choose?

5. What is your idea of the perfect morning?

6. You just got a job at the zoo. What animal do you want to take care of? Why?

7. If you could receive one luxury service every day for one year, what would you choose?

8. If you could read the diary of a famous person from history, who would you choose and why?

9. What is one thing you do every day you wish you did not have to do?

10. Wow! You just had quadruplets! Two boys and two girls! What are you going to name them?

11. What three things need to happen for you to have a really great day?

12. What three things need to happen for you to have a completely lousy day?

13. Who was the kindest person you ever met?

14. Name one thing you did between the ages of 6 and 12 that, looking back, you can't believe you did.

15. What was the most important day of your life? Why?

16. What are the four best personal qualities demonstrated by your parents?

17. What fairy tale (like "Jack in the Beanstalk") or fable (like "The Grasshopper and the Ants") best represents your life?

18. What is the most courageous thing you have ever done?

19. What was the most difficult thing about your adolescent years?

20. Describe a time when you were able to do something important only because of your faith.

Listening Test

A good skill for any group to learn is the art of listening. Take a moment to record your answers to the questions below and then tally up your score. Share your score with your group or share your impressions of your listening skills.

1. I frequently change the subject when it's my turn to talk.

A	B	C	D	E
Always	Frequently	Sometimes	Rarely	Never

2. I will interrupt someone if I have something I want to say.

A	B	C	D	E
Always	Frequently	Sometimes	Rarely	Never

3. After someone has spoken to me, I briefly summarize what they said, demonstrating I heard them.

A	B	C	D	E
Always	Frequently	Sometimes	Rarely	Never

4. I am likely to fidget with something (pen, hair, etc.) while someone is talking.

A	B	C	D	E
Always	Frequently	Sometimes	Rarely	Never

5. I avoid eye contact when someone is talking to me.

A	B	C	D	E
Always	Frequently	Sometimes	Rarely	Never

6. I purposefully ask questions which encourage someone to continue telling me about their topic.

A	B	C	D	E
Always	Frequently	Sometimes	Rarely	Never

7. When someone tells me about a problem, I tend to give advice and try and solve their problem, even though they do not specifically ask for my input.

A	B	C	D	E
Always	Frequently	Sometimes	Rarely	Never

8. In most conversations, I usually talk about myself.

A	B	C	D	E
Always	Frequently	Sometimes	Rarely	Never

9. I strive to demonstrate my empathy when someone is talking to me about their concerns.

A	B	C	D	E
Always	Frequently	Sometimes	Rarely	Never

10. When someone is talking to me, I think about what I am going to say next.

A	B	C	D	E
Always	Frequently	Sometimes	Rarely	Never

11. I roll my eyes, laugh or make jokes when someone says something incorrect, embarrassing or revealing.

A	B	C	D	E
Always	Frequently	Sometimes	Rarely	Never

12. I assure people that they are free to tell me anything.

A	B	C	D	E
Always	Frequently	Sometimes	Rarely	Never

13. When someone tells me about a problem, I'm likely to say, "I know just what you're going through."

A	B	C	D	E
Always	Frequently	Sometimes	Rarely	Never

14. I frequently say "yes," "uh-huh," "yeah" or something similar while someone is talking to me.

A	B	C	D	E
Always	Frequently	Sometimes	Rarely	Never

15. I try not to let my immediate tasks or concerns keep me from being available to listen to someone.

A	B	C	D	E
Always	Frequently	Sometimes	Rarely	Never

16. When someone hesitates while they are talking, I try to finish their sentences for them.

A	B	C	D	E
Always	Frequently	Sometimes	Rarely	Never

17. I might scold someone if what they tell me makes me feel uncomfortable.

A	B	C	D	E
Always	Frequently	Sometimes	Rarely	Never

18. I tell people that I am there if they need to be listened to.

A	B	C	D	E
Always	Frequently	Sometimes	Rarely	Never

SCORING: On questions 3, 6, 9, 12, 15 and 18 give yourself 5 points for each "A," 4 points for each "B," 3 points for each "C," 2 points for each "D" and 1 point for each "E." For the other questions, give yourself 1 point for each "A," 2 points for each "B," 3 points for each "C," 4 points for each "D" and 5 points for each "E." Higher scores indicate better listening skills.

Group Machine

Your group has unbelievable potential and can accomplish amazing things if everyone will work together for a common purpose. To demonstrate this, build a group machine. Select one of the machines listed below and work together to become that machine. Each person will need to be part of the machine. Happy building!

Old-time washing machine

Auto assembly line

Computer

Sausage-making machine

Car engine

Helicopter

Car wash

Diaper-changing machine

Steam train

Grandfather clock

Jukebox

Vending machine

Lawn mower

Pipe organ

Group Covenant

Any group can benefit by creating a group covenant. Reserve some time during one of the first meetings to discuss answers to the following questions. When everyone in the group has the same expectations for the group, everything runs more smoothly.

1. The purpose of our group is:

2. The goals of our group are:

3. We will meet for _____ weeks, after which we will decide if we wish to continue as a group. If we do decide to continue, we will reconsider this covenant.

4. We will meet _____ (weekly, every other week, monthly).

5. Our meetings will begin at _____ o'clock and we will strive to start and end on time.

6. We will meet at _____ or rotate from house to house.

7. We will take care of the following details:
   ❐ child care:
   ❐ refreshments:
   ❐ parking:

8. We agree to the following ground rules for our group:
   ❐ PRIORITY: While we are in this group we will give group meetings priority.
   ❐ PARTICIPATION: Everyone is given the right to their own opinion and all questions are respected.
   ❐ CONFIDENTIALITY: Anything said in the meeting is not to be repeated outside the meeting.
   ❐ EMPTY CHAIR: The group stays open to new people as long as group size and space requirements allow.
   ❐ SUPPORT: Permission is given to call each other in times of need.
   ❐ MINISTRY PROJECT: We agree to choose and complete a ministry project.
   ❐ ADVICE GIVING: Unsolicited advice giving is not allowed.

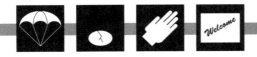

Prayer Methods

There are a variety of ways for a group of people to pray together. How the group chooses to pray depends greatly on what each person is comfortable with. Some people, for example, might not feel comfortable praying out loud in a group. Use this list to choose a method for prayer best suited for your group. The following suggestions for different ways to pray include a full spectrum of ideas. The list begins with "low risk" methods anyone will feel comfortable with and ends with suggestions which involve each person praying aloud.

1. Let a previously assigned leader close the group in prayer. The prayer might include thanking God for the opportunity to meet together, offering praise and thanks to God, praying about situations in anyone's life that might have been shared during the meeting, and asking God's help with applying the message of the discussion. Encourage each person to pray for one another in the coming week.

2. Read a prayer together such as the Lord's Prayer (Matt. 6:9–13), Paul's prayer for the Ephesians (Eph. 3:14–21) or the "Serenity Prayer":

    "Lord, grant us the serenity to accept the things we cannot control,
    the courage to change the things we can,
    and the wisdom to know the difference. Amen."

3. Ask the group to share their answers to the question, "How can we pray for you this week?" Remind the group that answering the question is optional. Have a previously assigned leader pray for the different prayer concerns. Asking for prayer concerns based on the discussion topic is always a good idea.

4. Form "prayer partners." Ask the group to share their prayer concerns, perhaps answering the question, "How can we help you in prayer this week?" Then group members are paired up and asked to pray for one another during the coming week. The leader or other previously assigned person can close the meeting with prayer.

5. Ask for prayer requests and then pray for one another silently. You can even ask the group members to pray silently for the person on their right or left. The leader or other previously assigned person closes the prayer time by praying aloud.

6. Ask the group to share their prayer concerns, then ask for volunteers to pray for each prayer concern. This is a good way to encourage your group to begin praying aloud for one another. For example, if Jethro requests prayer

for his ailing donkey, the leader might ask the group, "Who will pray for Jethro's donkey?" The actual prayer time is done with the group standing or seated in a circle. The leader can begin the prayer time, telling the group to pray in turn, going around the circle either clockwise or counter-clockwise. Or the leader can pray briefly for each person and then pause to let the volunteer add their prayer for that person.

7. Sentence prayers are another great way to help your group learn to pray aloud. During your prayer time, ask each person to take turns completing one of the following sentences:

> *"Lord, I want to praise you for ..."*
> *"Lord, show me what to do about ..."*
> *"Lord, I want to thank you for ..."*
> *"Lord, please help someone I love ..."*

8. When everyone in the group is comfortable praying aloud, you can ask each person to pray for the person on their right or left. This can even be done silently if a person chooses not to pray aloud. For best results, the group should hold hands, gently squeezing the hand of the person next to them when they have finished praying. Or each person can say "Amen" when they have finished praying. The leader closes the prayer time when everyone has had a chance to pray.

9. A group can also pray topically. For example, the leader might say, "Lord, hear our prayers of praise and thanksgiving." Then everyone who chooses can pray accordingly. Other introductory prayer statements include:

> *"Lord, hear our prayers for one another."*
> *"Lord, hear our prayers of confession."*
> *"Lord, hear our prayers for our church."*
> *" Lord, here our prayers for people we know who do not follow you."*

Prayer Form

This Soft Landing is a creative way to help people express themselves to God and to one another. Each person fills in the four blanks from the lists below. Then, during the prayer time, each person reads what they have chosen and continues their prayer accordingly. Use this activity once everyone in the group is comfortable praying aloud, or let anyone who chooses pray silently.

"_____   _____
                    column 1   column 2

      |_____
                      column 3

_____ ..."
                          column 4

Column 1	**Column 2**	**Column 3**
Dear	God	Humbly
Holy	Father	Eagerly
Magnificent	Savior	Joyfully
Almighty	Lord	Finally
Heavenly	Master	Reluctantly
Sovereign	King	Solemnly
Loving	Lamb	Cheerfully
Gracious	Redeemer	Enthusiastically
Precious	Deliverer	Obediently

Column 4

Praise you for ...
Thank you for ...
Remember what you have done for me ...
Exalt you because ...
Confess my sins ...
Lift up a loved one ...
Pray for someone who needs your love ...
Need you to ...
Ask for your guidance ...

Guess Who?

This is a fun game that takes a little while, but it is a valuable way to close a meeting. One person leaves the room and then one of the remaining people is chosen. The rest of the group selects one of the sentences below which describes the "chosen" person. After everyone has chosen a sentence that describes the "chosen" person (the "chosen" person also needs to select a sentence to describe himself or herself), the person who left the room returns and everyone takes turns sharing their sentence. After everyone has finished, the person who left the room tries to guess who the group is describing.

"If this person was a _____, they would be ..."

color
planet
literary character
car
historical figure
country
precious stone
animal
weather phenomena
holiday
cartoon character
movie
song
painting
toy

The Wonderful Game

This Soft Landing is a fun way for a group to affirm one another. Begin by writing the names of your group members in the blanks on the left side of the page. Fill in the names in the order of where each person is sitting, starting clockwise with the person on your left. Then complete the sentences, for example, "If *Michael* was a book, he would be *The World Book Encyclopedia* because *he knows about so many things*." When everyone is finished, take turns sharing your answers.

If _____ was a book, he/she would be _____ because ...

If _____ was an aircraft, he/she would be _____ because ...

If _____ was a museum, he/she would be _____ because ...

If _____ was furniture, he/she would be _____ because ...

If _____ was a flower, he/she would be _____ because ...

If _____ was a sports hero, he/she would be _____ because ...

If _____ was a building, he/she would be _____ because ...

If _____ was a circus performer, he/she would be _____ because ...

If _____ was a comic, he/she would be _____ because ...

If _____ was a super hero, he/she would be _____ because ...

If _____ was a tree, he/she would be _____ because ...

If _____ was a famous painting, he/she would be _____ because ...

If _____ was a dessert, he/she would be _____ because ...

If _____ was a sea creature, he/she would be _____ because ...

If _____ was a TV star, he/she would be _____ because ...

If _____ was a toy, he/she would be _____ because ...

If _____ was a farm animal, he/she would be _____ because ...

If _____ was a car, he/she would be _____ because ...

Match the Member

Your group members have a tremendous variety of qualities and strengths. If you could choose how you would like to spend time with your group members, what would you like to do? In the blank lines on the right, list your group members in any order. Then match each group member with the activities on the left. Draw a line between the group member and the activity you would like to do with them. Then take turns sharing your choices with the group.

Spend two weeks on a deserted island   _____

Have on my side during an argument   _____

Be there for me when the bottom drops out   _____

Call me when I feel sad or discouraged   _____

Help me through a spiritual crisis   _____

Take on a picnic   _____

Play miniature golf or something childlike   _____

Help me with a major decision   _____

Listen when I confess something I've done   _____

Help me dream, plan big and reach my potential   _____

Go shopping with   _____

Observe when I need an example   _____

Help me plan a party   _____

Write my biography   _____

Help me fix my car   _____

Go with me to tell someone about Jesus   _____

Help me consider the value of a new venture   _____

Join me on a mountain-climbing trip   _____

Loving Others

Your church should be a place of tremendous love among the members. Many consider the church a place where love can be learned and then taken into the rest of our relationships. There are many ways church members, even members of your group, can love one another. Consider the list below. Which of the following ways can you use to love the people in your church this week? What about the people in your group? Who do you know who needs to be loved with one of the ways listed here? Finally, of all the ways of being loved, how would you like to be loved this week? (Perhaps someone in your group will make your wish come true!) Take turns sharing your answers to these questions.

Ask someone how you can PRAY FOR THEM.

Clearly let someone know that you will ACCEPT THEM no matter what they need to say or do.

Ask someone what you could do to ENCOURAGE THEM.

Tell someone how they have INSPIRED YOU.

Tell someone how you have seen JESUS AT WORK in their life.

Tell someone you ADMIRE THEIR LISTENING SKILLS.

Send someone a CARD or LETTER.

Ask someone ABOUT THEIR LIFE, such as how their job, schoolwork or project is going.

Confide in someone, trusting them enough to SHARE YOUR PRAYER CONCERNS with them.

Share an inspirational SCRIPTURE with someone.

THANK someone for their contribution to the church.

Tell someone you WANT TO LISTEN to whatever they need to talk about.

Tell someone how much you appreciate them sharing THEIR SPIRITUAL GIFTS to strengthen the church.

Ask if you can HELP SOMEONE'S EFFORTS to share Christ's love or explain the Gospel to others.

Ask someone if they need ANY ASSISTANCE with a task or problem.

Ask someone about their FAMILY.

CALL someone just to say "hello!"

ASK someone "How's it going?" and then ask, *"Really,* how's it going?"

BRING SOMEONE FLOWERS when they are sad or under the weather.

Tell someone how you are PRAYING FOR THEM and ask how else you could pray for them.

SUBMIT to someone with all humility and love.

Go to someone you've wronged and ask them for their FORGIVENESS.

TELL someone that you are enriched when they attend and contribute to the worship service.

CALL someone who was unable to attend the worship service and tell them about the service.

CONFRONT someone, in a loving way, with something they need to hear.

PRAY for someone in a thoughtful, specific way.

Make a GIFT BASKET for someone, full of their favorite food—and include some inspirational items.

Use your ARTS AND CRAFTS skills to make something for someone.

TREAT someone to breakfast, coffee, lunch, dinner or ice cream.

Seven Great Decisions

One of the best ways to take advantage of an inspiring meeting is make some positive decisions about your life. Use the weekly calendar below to record seven great decisions about your life, one for each day of the week. After you have decided on the improvements you are going to make, take turns sharing your decisions with the group. Your group might choose to follow-up with one another at your next meeting to see how successful you were at fulfilling your seven great decisions.

SELF-CARE SUNDAY: One thing I'm going to do to take care of myself:

MEDICAL MONDAY: One thing I'm going to do to improve my health:

TREASURE TUESDAY: One thing I'm going to do to improve my financial situation:

WORKING WEDNESDAY: One thing I'm going to do to be Christlike at my job or during my daily activities:

THOUGHTFUL THURSDAY: One thing I'm going to do to surprise someone with kindness:

FAMILY FRIDAY: One thing I'm going to do to improve my relationships with family members:

SPIRITUAL SATURDAY: One thing I'm going to do to enhance my spiritual life:

Spiritual R$_x$

Every now and then we get sick. Sometimes we get sick spiritually, emotionally or relationally. What "prescription" do you need for your spiritual ailment? Go to your spiritual medicine cabinet and choose a Bible verse that will help you find the healing you need. Take turns sharing with your group what passage you have chosen and why. (Note: Each person will need access to a Bible for this activity.)

Anger

James 1:19–20
Ecclesiastes 7:9
Proverbs 14:17
Proverbs 15:18
Proverbs 22:24–25
Ephesians 4:26
Matthew 5:22

Grief

Psalm 23
1 Corinthians 15:55
Romans 5:9
Hebrews 2:14–15
John 8:51
Psalm 48:14
Romans 8:38–39

Jealousy

Deuteronomy 5:21
James 3:16
James 4:5
Ecclesiastes 4:4
Proverbs 23:17–18
Proverbs 14:30

Loneliness

John 14:18
Isaiah 58:9
2 Corinthians 6:18
Genesis 28:15
Psalm 40:17
Psalm 139:1–10
Matthew 28:19–20

Forgiveness

Ephesians 4:31–32
1 John 1:9
Luke 17:3–4
Mark 11:25
Isaiah 1:18
Psalm 51
Matthew 6:14–15
Matthew 18:23–35

Fear

Luke 12:32
Mark 4:40
Isaiah 41:13
Proverbs 1:33
2 Timothy 1:7
Proverbs 3:24
1 Peter 3:12–14
Romans 8:15
John 14:27
Psalm 27:1–3
Psalm 27:14

Fruit of the Spirit

Each believer reflects the Spirit of God in Christlike ways. In his letter to the Galatians, Paul tells that church the kind of behavior they should exhibit as Christians.

But the fruit of the Spirit is love, joy, peace, patience, kindness, goodness, faithfulness, gentleness and self-control.   Galatians 5:22–23

Which of the following "fruit of the Spirit" have you noticed among your group members? Write each group member's name on the blanks and then match the fruit you have seen in their life. Take turns sharing your answers with the group.

_____ LOVING LIMEADE: You are sweet and refreshing, always satisfying others.

_____ JOY JAM: You spread happiness and joy on everything you say and do.

_____ PEACE COBBLER: A serving of you and everything is all right in the world.

_____ PLUM PATIENCE: You're plum patient when it comes to waiting for God.

_____ KINDNESS KANTELOUPE: We've all enjoyed a slice of your thoughtfulness.

_____ GOODNESS GRAPEFRUIT: You set an example for us with your behavior.

_____ FAITHFULNESS FRUIT SALAD: You live as though you know God is present.

_____ GENTLE GIANT WATERMELON: You're big-hearted as you consider others' feelings.

_____ SEEDLESS SELF-CONTROL: You have so much control you can stop after just one grape!

I Wish I Had ...

Everyone in your group has wonderful qualities. What qualities of each person do you admire? What qualities of each person do you wish you could have? In the blanks on the left write down the names of all the people in your group. In the blanks on the right, write one quality of that person you wish you had. Take turns sharing your answers with the group.

Group Member   **Quality I Wish I Had:**

_____   _____

_____   _____

_____   _____

_____   _____

_____   _____

_____   _____

_____   _____

_____   _____

_____   _____

I See You As ...

Over time, you learn many wonderful things about your group members. Eventually, you will be able to see ways they can serve God. Look over the list below and write down the names of the people in your group next to the task you can see them doing and enjoying. This activity will help you affirm the strengths of your group members and help each person see how others view their strengths. Take turns sharing your answers. (Note: This list of ministry possibilities is adopted from Leadership Training Network's *Starter Kit for Mobilizing Ministry,* 1994).

_____ career guides for the homeless   _____ trustee

_____ Scripture reader for shut-ins   _____ usher

_____ dance team worship   _____ elder

_____ Sunday morning receptionist   _____ banner-maker

_____ plant grower for hospital patients   _____ small group leader

_____ new Christian mentor   _____ small group host

_____ host family for unwed mothers   _____ acolyte coordinator

_____ disaster relief volunteer   _____ new visitor contact

_____ parking lot attendant   _____ adult Bible teacher

_____ stewardship committee   _____ bus driver

_____ helper for single-parent families   _____ youth leader

_____ children's Bible teacher   _____ youth chaperone

_____ food coordinator for bereaved   _____ greeter

_____ baby holders and rockers   _____ church librarian

_____ handbell choir member   _____ small group coach

_____ "Mop and Hammer" team   _____ new member guide

_____ blood drive coordinator   _____ seminar organizer

_____ gifts assessment mentor   _____ hospital visitor

_____ prayer team coordinator   _____ door-to-door visitation

_____ grief support group leader   _____ church grounds crew

_____ Vacation Bible School teacher   _____ church board member

_____ Scripture-memory coordinator   _____ prison ministry

_____ crisis phone line counselor

_____ recovery ministry spokesperson

_____ addict support program team

_____ tape ministry coordinator

_____ marketplace evangelism team

_____ spiritual renewal retreat director

_____ meals-on-wheels driver

_____ medical and dental advisor

_____ foreign mission advocate

_____ sports and recreation director

_____ church information center attendant

_____ nursing home ministry coordinator

_____ outreach ministry to minority groups

_____ church newsletter layout specialist

_____ intergenerational ministry director

_____ caregiver for children of divorce

_____ Habitat for Humanity coordinator

_____ holiday sanctuary decoration team

_____ new ministries assessment director

_____ church office administrative assistant

_____ crisis pregnancy center counselor

_____ Sunday school discussion leader

_____ serve on a committee or ministry team

_____ mechanic for confused car owners

_____ special events team

_____ choir

_____ junior high mentor

_____ audiovisual assistant

_____ nursery worker

_____ ministry catalog editor

_____ church photographer

_____ church bookstore clerk

_____ video camera operator

C.E.O.

Congratulations! You have been elected the Chief Executive Officer of Acme Amalgamated, Inc.! Your first responsibility is to choose your high-level executives. Who do you want to lead the different departments in your new company? Choose different group members to fill the different positions in Acme Amalgamated and then take turns sharing your choices with the group.

_____ VICE PRESIDENT: This person is the perfect choice to be my right-hand man or woman for big decisions and important projects.

_____ DIRECTOR OF MARKETING: This person is the obvious choice for doing a great job telling people about our products.

_____ OFFICE MANAGER: Here is someone who can keep things running smoothly, efficiently organized and with high productivity.

_____ DIRECTOR OF HUMAN RESOURCES: With tremendous people skills, this person is great at helping others find fulfillment.

_____ LEGAL COUNSEL: This person is intelligent and shrewd, able to keep justice a priority in everything we do.

_____ PUBLIC RELATIONS: With tremendous social skills, this person puts his or her best food forward and presents a wonderful image.

_____ DIRECTOR OF FINANCIAL OPERATIONS: Here is someone who is extremely well-organized and focused enough to keep an eye on the details.

_____ CHAIRMAN OF THE BOARD: This person is the ideal choice to oversee my life and be a mentor for me.

_____ DIRECTOR OF RESEARCH: Fantastic creativity and a way of seeing things the rest of us can't are valuable qualities of this person.

Warm Fuzzies

When was the last time you gave someone a "warm fuzzy"? A warm fuzzy is a term used to describe saying or doing something for someone that made them feel good. From the list below (or come up with your own) think of the warm fuzzies you would like to give to the people in your group. Or have each person give a warm fuzzy to the person on their right or left.

Box of Puppies
So you will be overwhelmed with warm bundles of joy.

Flannel Business Suit
So you will know, wherever you are, that you are special.

Cashmere Sweater
So you could go anywhere and be surrounded by warmth.

Teddy Bear
So you can snuggle with something soft and friendly when you feel sad or alone.

Big, Chubby Cat
So you can always cuddle with a furry friend.

Cap and Mittens
So no matter how cold the world gets, you will always be safe and warm.

Puffy Down Comforter
So you can rest peacefully, surrounded by comfort.

Big, Fluffy Slippers
So your feet will be happy after you walk the extra mile for others.

Beanbag Chair
So you can relax after a busy day and disappear in comfort.

Bible Characters

The people in your group are amazing, just like the people in the Bible! They have wonderful faith and glorify God in many exciting ways. Affirm the people in your group by matching them with one of the Bible characters listed below. Go around the group and match each person or match the person on your right or left. Take turns sharing your answers.

NOAH (Genesis 6–9): You have the tremendous ability to use your faith to protect others from harm.

MOSES (Exodus 2–20): Your faith gives you the amazing ability to lead others.

MARY (Luke 1:26–56): Despite your touching humility, your faith makes you available to God's plans.

PETER (Acts 2–4): We have all enjoyed watching your faith grow and progress so wonderfully.

ESTHER (the book of Esther): Your faith gives you an inner beauty that makes you shine in any situation.

PHOEBE (Romans 16:1–2): Your love for others and service to them shows your faith to us all.

JOB (the book of Job): Your faith has stood strong even when you faced painful struggles.

PRISCILLA (Acts 18): Your faith is seen by your intelligent and inspiring understanding of the Bible.

ABRAHAM (Genesis 12–22): Your faith makes you devoted to the point of sacrificing anything to obey God.

PAUL (Acts 19–20): Your profound love for the church shows us the substance of your faith.

SOLOMON (1 Kings 3–4): Your faith has given you incredible wisdom which we enjoy so much.

JAMES (the book of James): Your faith is obvious because you say what we need to hear.

DEBORAH (Judges 4–5): Your impressive ability to guide and inspire clearly demonstrates your faith.

JOSEPH (Genesis 37–50): You have a faith that always seems to help you rise to the top.

THE CENTURION (Matthew 8:5–13): Your strong faith stands out even in a culture that does not appreciate it.

RUTH (the book of Ruth): You have a wonderful way of caring for others because of your faith.

THE MAGI (Matthew 2:1–12): Your faith is evident because it is obvious that you will go to any lengths to find Jesus.

Self-Esteem

It is our lifelong privilege to learn to see ourselves with the same love and worthiness that God sees us. Choose one of the verses below that helps you look at yourself through God's eyes and enhances your self-esteem. Then take turns sharing the verse you chose and why. You might choose to memorize the verse you have chosen and recite the verse at your next meeting.

I praise you because I am fearfully and wonderfully made; your works are wonderful, I know that full well. Psalm 139:14

"The Lord your God is with you, he is mighty to save. He will take great delight in you, he will quiet you with his love, he will rejoice over you with singing." Zephaniah 3:17

He answered: " 'Love the Lord your God with all your heart and with all your soul and with all your strength and with all your mind'; and, 'Love your neighbor as yourself.' " Luke 10:27

How great is the love the Father has lavished on us, that we should be called children of God! And that is what we are! The reason the world does not know us is that it did not know him. 1 John 3:1

Therefore, as God's chosen people, holy and dearly loved, clothe yourselves with compassion, kindness, humility, gentleness and patience. Colossians 3:12

But you are a chosen people, a royal priesthood, a holy nation, a people belonging to God, that you may declare the praises of him who called you out of darkness into his wonderful light. 1 Peter 2:9

So God created man in his own image, in the image of God he created him; male and female he created them. ... God saw all that he had made, and it was very good. And there was evening, and there was morning—the sixth day. Genesis 1:27,31

"As the Father has loved me, so have I loved you. Now remain in my love." John 15:9

The Lord appeared to us in the past, saying: "I have loved you with an everlasting love; I have drawn you with loving-kindness." Jeremiah 31:3

And I pray that you, being rooted and established in love, may have power, together with all the saints, to grasp how wide and long and high and deep is the love of Christ, and to know this love that surpasses knowledge—that you may be filled to the measure of all the fullness of God. Ephesians 3:17b–19

Body of Christ

Your church is a living body of Christ, composed of all the members of your congregation who reveal his Spirit in their lives. How do the members of your group fit in the body of Christ? What is their special contribution to Christ's presence in your church? Affirm your group members by choosing which function of the body of Christ they serve. Either go in a circle, with each person identifying the contribution of the person on their right or left, or go around the group taking turns as each person listens while the rest of the group shares the contribution they see in that person.

HANDS: You reveal Jesus by the special skills you can do for others that they cannot do for themselves.

BACK: Your faith is strong because you hold up to crises, fear and doubt, reminding those around you that Jesus is near.

SHOULDERS: You show us Christ's gentleness by being the kind of person we can go to when we need a shoulder to cry on.

FEET: You go where God sends you to share Christ's love with others. You take your faith places.

MOUTH: Just like Jesus, you say what needs to be said to comfort, encourage and challenge.

EYES: You have the eyes of Christ because you can share his compassion in the way you look at someone.

EARS: You show love and respect for someone through your Christlike listening skills.

KNEES: As a prayer warrior, you demonstrate Jesus' reliance on prayer through your devotion to God.

ARMS: You use your arms to embrace people and comfort them just like Jesus did.

LEGS: You have the courage to stand up for what you believe in, even when it isn't popular.

Heavenly Hope

Living with the hope of our eternal life is a foundation of the Christian life. Knowing that our future is with God is indescribably comforting. Choose one of the verses below that brings you hope and then take turns sharing which verse you chose and why. You might decide to memorize the verse you have chosen and recite the verse at your next meeting.

Jesus said to her, "I am the resurrection and the life. He who believes in me will live, even though he dies; and whoever lives and believes in me will never die. Do you believe this?"
John 11:25–26

For the Lord himself will come down from heaven, with a loud command, with the voice of the archangel and with the trumpet call of God, and the dead in Christ will rise first.
1 Thessalonians 4:16

He will wipe every tear from their eyes. There will be no more death or mourning or crying or pain, for the old order of things has passed away.
Revelation 21:4

"And after my skin has been destroyed, yet in my flesh I will see God; I myself will see him with my own eyes—I, and not another. How my heart yearns within me!"
Job 19:26–27

Now we know that if the earthly tent we live in is destroyed, we have a building from God, an eternal house in heaven, not built by human hands.
2 Corinthians 5:1

"My sheep listen to my voice; I know them, and they follow me. I give them eternal life, and they shall never perish; no one can snatch them out of my hand."
John 10:27–28

Praise be to the God and Father of our Lord Jesus Christ! In his great mercy he has given us new birth into a living hope through the resurrection of Jesus Christ from the dead.
1 Peter 1:3

... the faith and love that spring from the hope that is stored up for you in heaven and that you have already heard about in the word of truth, the gospel that has come to you.
Colossians 1:5–6a

Listen, I tell you a mystery: We will not all sleep, but we will all be changed—in a flash, in the twinkling of an eye, at the last trumpet. For the trumpet will sound, the dead will be raised imperishable, and we will be changed.
1 Corinthians 15:51–52

Group Climate

What is the weather like in your group? Is it springtime in your group or winter? How would you describe the climate of your group? Answer the questions below to evaluate your group and then take turns sharing your answers. This Soft Landing can be used to help discuss any changes your group might need to make.

1. I would describe the WEATHER in our group as:
   ❐ hot and muggy—The summer doldrums have set in.
   ❐ cool and breezy—This group is refreshing and enjoyable to me.
   ❐ stormy—It's a little too turbulent in this group for my taste.
   ❐ rainy—I thrive on the heavenly blessings this group provides.
   ❐ snow in July—This group makes no sense to me.
   ❐ other:_____

2. I would describe the SEASON in our group as:
   ❐ winter—It's cold and dreary with the longest nights of the year.
   ❐ summer—It's hot outside and we're hot! Watch out! Here we come!
   ❐ spring—We're growing and blooming. Great things are on the way.
   ❐ fall—It's cool and leaves are falling, it might be time for our group to hibernate.
   ❐ other:_____

3. I would describe the ENVIRONMENT of our group as:

Swamp
It's scary here with many unseen dangers.

Barren Desert
As I look around all I can see for miles and miles is ... nothing.

Alpine Meadow
The air is clear and the meadows are blooming.

Stormy Coastline
Raise the hurricane flag, trouble's brewing.

Lunar Landscape
It's interesting here but we're separated by our spacesuits.

Epic Vista
Here I can see things I usually can't see.

Group Affirmation

Affirming each other is a great thing, and so is affirming the group as a whole. As each member of your group has their own strengths and gifts, your group has a personality all its own. Choose one of the items below which best describes how you feel about your group and take turns sharing your choices with one another.

Harlem Globetrotters
We mystify everyone with our synchronization, and have a ball doing it!

Moscow Ballet Company
We perform with beauty and elegance inspiring everyone who sees us.

Flying Foodinis
Our group seems like a trapeze act, yet we hold each other up.

U.S. Coast Guard Search and Rescue
We are an incredible team who helps others in distress.

Sistine Chapel Restoration Team
With hard work and friendship, we make God's presence more real.

Blue Angels Aerobatic Team
We work together with awesome skill and precision.

Country Hoedown Square Dancers
We move like clockwork with everyone involved, and have lots of fun.

National Forest Service Firefighters
We'll go through the flames together to accomplish our goals.

New York Philharmonic
We each play our part and make beautiful music together.

Chess Pieces
Each of us has a clearly defined purpose in the contest we are in.

114

God's Will

Sometimes identifying God's will for our lives can be difficult. Choose one of the verses below that comforts you in your search for God's will and then take turns sharing the verse you chose and why. You might decide to memorize the verse you have chosen and recite the verse at your next meeting.

Thomas said to him, "Lord, we don't know where you are going, so how can we know the way?" Jesus answered, "I am the way and the truth and the life. No one comes to the Father except through me."   *John 14:5–6*

"For I know the plans I have for you," declares the Lord, "plans to prosper you and not to harm you, plans to give you hope and a future."   *Jeremiah 29:11*

Whether you turn to the right or to the left, your ears will hear a voice behind you, saying, "This is the way; walk in it."   *Isaiah 30:21*

For this God is our God for ever and ever; he will be our guide even to the end.
                                                                                Psalm 48:14

In his heart a man plans his course, but the Lord determines his steps.
                                                                            Proverbs 16:9

Trust in the Lord with all your heart and lean not on your own understanding; in all your ways acknowledge him, and he will make your paths straight.
                                                                             Proverbs 3:6

I will instruct you and teach you in the way you should go; I will counsel you and watch over you.   *Psalm 32:8*

I will lead the blind by ways they have not known, along unfamiliar paths I will guide them; I will turn the darkness into light before them and make the rough places smooth. These are the things I will do; I will not forsake them.
                                                                              Isaiah 42:16

You guide me with your counsel, and afterward you will take me into glory.
                                                                              Psalm 73:24

Now listen, you who say, "Today or tomorrow we will go to this or that city, spend a year there, carry on business and make money." Why, you do not even know what will happen tomorrow. What is your life? You are a mist that appears for a little while and then vanishes. Instead, you ought to say, "If it is the Lord's will, we will live and do this or that."   *James 4:13–15*

Brainstorm

Jesus demonstrated the importance of ministering to people. Sometimes our church groups lose perspective on the importance of hands-on ministry for the sake of others. Many groups decide to do a ministry project in addition to their other purposes. Use this activity as a guide to help your group discuss a ministry project. Take turns sharing your "passion" for the different stages of life, basic needs and special conditions. Share your ideas and dreams with the group and then work together to reach a consensus for a ministry project.

1. Are we ready for a ministry project?

2. What should our time commitment be to this project?
   ❐ a one-time project
   ❐ a short-term project
   ❐ a long-term project
   ❐ a continual project

3. Who should we help?
   ❐ one another
   ❐ people in our church
   ❐ people in our community

4. What needs in people's lives should we strive to meet?

Stage of Life	Basic Need	Special Conditions
Infants	Shelter	Spiritually lost
Children	Food	Poor or homeless
Teenagers	Clothing	Physically ill
Young adults	Love/nurture	Physically disabled
Middle-aged	Cleanliness	Emotional distress
Elderly	Safety	Substance addiction
Families	Sense of purpose	Family problems
Any age	Job training	Broken families
Other:	Other:	Other:

5. How could our group do this project "in Jesus' name"?

God and Money

Money and success are important pursuits in our culture. The Bible frequently tells us the importance of keeping money in perspective and what true success really is. Choose one of the verses below that is most meaningful to you. Then take turns sharing which verse you chose and why. You might decide to memorize the verse you have chosen and recite the verse at your next meeting.

Do not wear yourself out to get rich; have the wisdom to show restraint. Cast but a glance at riches, and they are gone, for they will surely sprout wings and fly off to the sky like an eagle.
Proverbs 23:4–5

Listen, my dear brothers: Has not God chosen those who are poor in the eyes of the world to be rich in faith and to inherit the kingdom he promised those who love him?
James 2:5

Command them to do good, to be rich in good deeds, and to be generous and willing to share.
1 Timothy 6:18

They will throw their silver into the streets, and their gold will be an unclean thing. Their silver and gold will not be able to save them in the day of the Lord's wrath. They will not satisfy their hunger or fill their stomachs with it, for it has made them stumble into sin.
Ezekiel 7:19

Moreover, when God gives any man wealth and possessions, and enables him to enjoy them, to accept his lot and be happy in his work—this is a gift of God.
Ecclesiastes 5:19

"No servant can serve two masters. Either he will hate the one and love the other, or he will be devoted to the one and despise the other. You cannot serve both God and Money."
Luke 16:13

Wealth and riches are in his house, and his righteousness endures forever.
Psalm 112:3

For the love of money is a root of all kinds of evil. Some people, eager for money, have wandered from the faith and pierced themselves with many griefs.
1 Timothy 6:10

I have learned the secret of being content in any and every situation, whether well fed or hungry, whether living in plenty or in want. I can do everything through him who gives me strength.
Philippians 4:12–13

Movie Affirmation

Let your meeting land softly by recognizing the positive qualities of your group members that you have noticed during the time you've been together. Choose one of the movie types below that describes each person in your group and take turns affirming each person. Another way to use the affirmation activities is to draw names, then choose one movie affirmation, one nautical affirmation (p. 125) and one bird affirmation (p. 120) that describes the person whose name you drew. Then take turns sharing the affirmation qualities you chose and see if the group can guess whose name you drew.

Spy Thriller
You are adventurous and unpredictable. We never know what you are going to do next.

Action Adventure
Your no-nonsense approach and high-octane personality always makes life interesting.

Romance Classic
Leading with your heart, you remind us how wonderful love can be.

Rootin' Tootin' Western
You are rip snortin', rugged and down to earth, always keeping us entertained.

Sci-Fi Extravaganza
You have a wonderful imagination and exciting special effects.

Mysterious Who-dun-it
You are full of wonderful secrets and surprises.

Animation Classic
You are colorful and childlike, keeping us mesmerized with your hilarious capers.

Touching Drama
You are sensitive and expressive. You remind us of the beauty of the human spirit.

Fascinating Documentary
Your intelligence and curiosity enriches us all.

Jump for Joy

Joy is the constant awareness, regardless of the situation, that everything is in God's control. For the believer, joy exists beneath crises, bad days and rotten experience. But sometimes our joy needs a boost. Choose one of the verses below that speaks to your heart. Then take turns sharing which verse you chose and why. You might decide to memorize the verse you have chosen and recite the verse at your next meeting.

The ransomed of the Lord will return. They will enter Zion with singing; everlasting joy will crown their heads. Gladness and joy will overtake them, and sorrow and sighing will flee away.   *Isaiah 51:11*

You will go out in joy and be led in peace; the mountains and hills will burst into song before you, and all the trees of the field will clap their hands.   *Isaiah 55:12*

I delight greatly in the Lord; my soul rejoices in my God. For he has clothed me with garments of salvation and arrayed me in a robe of righteousness, as a bridegroom adorns his head like a priest, and as a bride adorns herself with her jewels.   *Isaiah 61:10*

Blessed are those who have learned to acclaim you, who walk in the light of your presence, O Lord. They rejoice in your name all day long; they exult in your righteousness.   *Psalm 89:15–16*

Shouts of joy and victory resound in the tents of the righteous: "The Lord's right hand has done mighty things!"   *Psalm 118:15*

You have filled my heart with greater joy than when their grain and new wine abound.   *Psalm 4:7*

Light is shed upon the righteous and joy on the upright in heart.   *Psalm 97:11*

"I have told you this so that my joy may be in you and that your joy may be complete."   *John 15:11*

"Now is your time of grief, but I will see you again and you will rejoice, and no one will take away your joy."   *John 16:22*

Though you have not seen him, you love him; and even though you do not see him now, you believe in him and are filled with an inexpressible and glorious joy, for you are receiving the goal of your faith, the salvation of your souls.

1 Peter 1:8

Bird Affirmation

What better way to close a meeting than to affirm the qualities you noticed in your fellow group members? Choose one of the birds below that describes each person in your group and take turns affirming each person. Another way to use the affirmation activities is to draw names, then choose one bird affirmation, one nautical affirmation (p. 125) and one movie affirmation (p. 118) that describes the person whose name you drew. Then take turns sharing the affirming qualities you chose and see if the group can guess whose name you drew.

Mockingbird
Your sweet spirit encourages everyone like the sweet song of a bird.

Owl
WHO is wiser than you? Your wisdom is a wonderful asset to our group.

Hawk
With your sharp eyes, you can see positive things about people the rest of us miss.

Dove
You seem to bring peace wherever you go, helping people through conflict.

San Diego Chicken
You have a lovable childlike spirit, entertaining us with your hilarious antics.

Swan
You carry yourself with great dignity, bringing elegance wherever you go.

Bat
When times are dark you have a way of showing us where to go.

Hummingbird
You have tremendous energy and accomplish the impossible, like flying backwards!

Peacock
You always surprise us with your unexpected color and brilliance.

Helping Others

Throughout the Scriptures, we are told the importance of helping others. Certainly Jesus demonstrated a life of compassion and action for the sake of the people around him. From the list below, choose a verse that is especially meaningful to you. Then take turns sharing which verse you chose and why. You might decide to memorize the verse you have chosen and recite the verse at your next meeting.

"They also will answer, 'Lord, when did we see you hungry or thirsty or a stranger or needing clothes or sick or in prison, and did not help you?' He will reply, 'I tell you the truth, whatever you did not do for one of the least of these, you did not do for me.' "
Matthew 25:44–45

All they asked was that we should continue to remember the poor, the very thing I was eager to do.
Galatians 2:10

Each man should give what he has decided in his heart to give, not reluctantly or under compulsion, for God loves a cheerful giver.
2 Corinthians 9:7

Suppose a brother or sister is without clothes and daily food. If one of you says to him, "Go, I wish you well; keep warm and well fed," but does nothing about his physical needs, what good is it?"
James 2:15–16

Do not forget to entertain strangers, for by so doing some people have entertained angels without knowing it.
Hebrews 13:2

If anyone has material possessions and sees his brother in need but has no pity on him, how can the love of God be in him?
1 John 3:17

"I tell you the truth, anyone who gives you a cup of water in my name because you belong to Christ will certainly not lose his reward."
Mark 9:41

"In everything I did, I showed you that by this kind of hard work we must help the weak, remembering the words the Lord Jesus himself said: 'It is more blessed to give than to receive.' "
Acts 20:35

Offer hospitality to one another without grumbling. Each one should use whatever gift he has received to serve others, faithfully administering God's grace in its various forms.
1 Peter 4:9–10

Crazy Ovations

Sometimes it's just plain fun to applaud and cheer each other. This Soft Landing includes a list of ways to show your love and appreciation to the people in your group. These ovations can be used in several ways. One way is to let each person choose how they would like to be cheered. Mildred, for example, might really enjoy being trumpeted by a room full of elephants. The group could also suggest ovations as different occasions present themselves. If Mildred finally remembers to bring refreshments to the meeting, the group might choose to give her a "Highbrow Hurrah."

STANDING OVATION: The honored person remains seated while the rest of the group stands up and claps for them. The seated person is free to say things like, "No, really ..." "You're too kind" or "Thank you, thank you."

STANDING "O": Instead of standing and clapping, the group stands, puts their arms over their heads like an "O" and says "Oooooooooooooooh" in unison.

GOLF CLAP: Understated, yet powerful, the golf clap is an affectionate expression. Each person simply claps quietly, as though they are at a golf tournament.

THE WAVE: If the fans at football stadiums can do the wave, your group can too. Beginning with everyone seated, the group goes around the circle, standing up, throwing their arms in the air and yelling.

HIP HIP HOORAY: This is a classic, but always heartwarming. The group shouts, "Hip Hip Hooray" in unison. The recipient of this ovation can request the number of "Hip Hip Hoorays" they would like to receive.

JOLLY GOOD FELLOW: Another classic, this is a great way to cheer someone, especially if the group can sing. The alternative lyrics are: "For she's a jolly good lady ..."

WHISTLE, STOMP AND CHEER: This is everything but clapping. The group simply expresses their feelings by making as much noise as possible.

FLYING SAUCER: Some folks might prefer this unusual cheer. Each person holds up their index finger, and makes a spiraling motion as they raise their finger higher and higher. This motion is accompanied by whatever flying saucer sound effect you can make. Repeat as necessary.

SEALS: One of the more popular animal cheers, this one involves each person barking and clapping like a seal in honor of the recipient. The bark is more like an "Ark!" and the clapping is done with the backs of the hands.

HIGHBROW HURRAH: This is a fun cheer. Everyone acts like they are at the opera or a poetry reading and instead of clapping, they shout "Bravo!" "Encore!" or "Speech!" Golf claps may be included. The recipient of this praise can feel free to bow several times and return for one or two curtain calls.

WATERMELON: This cheer involves pantomime and two sound effects. The cheer begins with each person pretending like they are quickly eating a big slice of watermelon. This action is accompanied by the appropriate slurping sound. Then everyone loudly spits out their imaginary seeds. The less enthusiastic or "reluctant praise" version of this cheer is called "The Cantaloupe."

KING OF THE ELEPHANTS: This is an ovation where everyone pretends they are an elephant and trumpets in honor of the person receiving the praise. To make this cheer effective, hold one arm in front of your face like a trunk and raise it while you trumpet.

COLLEGE CHEER: This cheer is limited only by the imagination of your group. You can change the words to fit your situation. Here is one example:

"Rah, rah, rus,
You're the one for us!
Rah, rah, roni,
You're the one and only!"

SNAPS: Some people like this way of cheering. Basically, instead of clapping, everyone snaps their fingers repeatedly. Go figure.

CRESCENDO: This is a way of applauding someone that will take most groups a few times to get right. Clapping begins very slowly, with one lone clap. This is followed by a few more until eventually the group is clapping like crazy.

OLD MacDONALD: Another animal cheer, "Old MacDonald" is an imaginary barnyard. Each person cheers by making the sound of a farm animal, such as a cow, horse, pig, donkey, goat, dog, duck, chicken, etc. In unison, everyone makes the sound of the animal they have chosen. Remember, there is a difference between oinking like a pig and oinking like a pig who is cheering someone.

Comfort During Troubles

Do you need comfort? God has promised to comfort us whenever we are feeling overwhelmed or struggling with something we cannot control. Choose one of the verses below that speaks to you and your situation. Then take turns sharing which verse you decide and why. You might decide to memorize the verse you have chosen and recite the verse at your next meeting.

For men are not cast off by the Lord forever. Though he brings grief, he will show compassion, so great is his unfailing love. For he does not willingly bring affliction or grief to the children of men. Lamentations 3:31–33

The Lord is my rock, my fortress and my deliverer; my God is my rock, in whom I take refuge. He is my shield and the horn of my salvation, my stronghold. Psalm 18:2

For he has not despised or disdained the suffering of the afflicted one; he has not hidden his face from him but has listened to his cry for help. Psalm 22:24

Wait for the Lord; be strong and take heart and wait for the Lord. Psalm 27:14

God is our refuge and strength, an ever-present help in trouble. Therefore we will not fear, though the earth give way and the mountains fall into the heart of the sea, though its waters roar and foam and the mountains quake with their surging. Psalm 46:1–3

Cast your cares on the Lord and he will sustain you; he will never let the righteous fall. Psalm 55:22

"I have told you these things, so that in me you may have peace. In this world you will have trouble. But taker heart! I have overcome the world." John 16:33

"Come to me, all you who are weary and burdened, and I will give you rest." Matthew 11:28

For just as the sufferings of Christ flow over into our lives, so also through Christ our comfort overflows 2 Corinthians 1:5

You are my hiding place; you will protect me from trouble and surround me with songs of deliverance. Psalm 32:7

Nautical Affirmation

Ahoy, Mates! Welcome to the U.S.S. Affirmation! Affirming one another is a great way for a group to encourage and love one another. An affirmation exercise is a great Soft Landing because we learn positive things about other group members during the course of the meetings. Choose one of the items below that describes each person in your group and take turns affirming each person. Another way to use the affirmation activities is to draw names, then choose one nautical affirmation, one movie affirmation (p. 118) and one bird affirmation (p. 120) that describes the person whose name you drew. Then take turns sharing the affirmation qualities you chose and see if the group can guess whose name you drew.

Chart
You have a way of showing us where we are and where we need to go.

Deep-Sea Diver
You move beyond the everyday and share your depth and wisdom with us.

Buoy
You lift our spirits as you share your wonderful faith with us.

Lighthouse
You let your light shine brightly, illuminating us with your wonderful spirit.

Harbor
Your gentle, loving ways makes you a place for us to go for safety and protection.

Full-Masted Clipper
You move through life with impressive dignity, powered by strong unseen winds.

Powerful Tug
You have strength and perseverance as you help us navigate our course.

Anchor
When storms and currents threaten to knock us off course, you hold us steady.

Fishing Net
You have a way of showing us what being a "fisher of men" really means.

Group Evaluation

When was the last time you had a checkup? Occasionally a group needs to stop and evaluate themselves. Take a few minutes to answer the following questions about your group. Take turns sharing your answers and discussing the results. Choose from the following answers for each question:

> 1 = not in a million years
> 2 = once in a blue moon
> 3 = about half the time
> 4 = most of the time
> 5 = always

1. I feel like this group values me as a person. 1 2 3 4 5

2. I feel like this group understands what I am
   trying to say. 1 2 3 4 5

3. This group interrupts or ignores my input. 1 2 3 4 5

4. I think this group has achieved its goals. 1 2 3 4 5

5. I think this group behaves toward me in a way
   that reveals Christ. 1 2 3 4 5

6. I feel like this group is able to accept my emotions. 1 2 3 4 5

7. This group is offering me relationships that are much
   more significant than my other relationships. 1 2 3 4 5

8. I think this group keeps things to themselves
   to avoid taking risks. 1 2 3 4 5

9. I feel like this group gives me the support I need. 1 2 3 4 5

10. I think this group encourages open discussion. 1 2 3 4 5

11. This group values everyone's contribution. 1 2 3 4 5

12. Our group does a good job with location, meeting
    space, refreshments, child care, etc. 1 2 3 4 5

First Aid

Christians are citizens of two realms. With one foot in the world and the other in the kingdom of God, we have yet to fully achieve the perfection Jesus offers us. In other words, we all make mistakes. Sometimes we make mistakes that can hurt others or even affect a group. Working through these mistakes and problems takes time and effort. If your group has had a conflict, or if feelings have been hurt or boundaries have been crossed, use this activity to help your group move beyond the situation. Many times a group can grow closer after they have worked through a problem together. Use these suggestions as a guideline. Remember that healing begins with listening.

✚ Go around the group and take turns sharing your feelings about what happened. Be sure to use "I" statements, such as "I felt hurt when ..." instead of "You were rude because ..." Talk about your own feelings, experiences and actions. After everyone has had a chance to speak, give everyone another opportunity to share. Repeat until everyone has said what they need to say regarding their feelings about what happened.

✚ Apologies are next. A group of believers and friends should be a safe place for people to admit when they were wrong and ask for forgiveness. The group should share in this, giving everyone an opportunity to acknowledge their inappropriate behavior or failure to respond properly.

✚ Give each person a chance to accept any apologies or say "thank you" for any apologies that have been offered. If someone does not feel as though the apologies respond adequately to their feelings, they are free to say, "I still feel ..." remembering to use "I" statements and discuss only their own feelings. In this case, additional apologies might be in order.

✚ Next, the group should discuss what ground rules or other changes, if any, the group should make to avoid similar problems. Too many rules can stifle open expression in a group, but reminding one another of considerate appropriate behavior can be valuable.

✚ The group should pray together. Holding hands during the prayer is a good idea. Pray for healing, love and unity. Give each person a chance to pray.

✚ End with a time of affirmation. Use one of the affirmation exercises in this book, or take turns affirming each person by completing this statement:

"A strength of yours I noticed through this situation is ..."

Easel

Where are your artistic skills, Leonardo? Actually, this activity is not an art show or drawing contest. This Soft Landing is a way for you to express your feelings for your group. How do you feel about your group? What has being in this group meant to you? How has this group affected your life? Draw your answer to these questions on the easel below and then take turns sharing your creation with the group.

Cheers!

Standing up to give a toast at an event is a wonderful tradition. Your group deserves the same honor. Write a toast to your group in the glass below that expresses how you feel about your group and the blessing you would like to bestow on them. When everyone has finished writing their toasts, give everyone a beverage and then take turns standing and sharing your toasts with the group.

Pack Your Suitcase

Saying good-bye is never easy. Sometimes groups need to say good-bye, even though everyone in the group will likely see each other again. This Soft Landing gives you a chance to make sure your group members will be well equipped as they continue their journey once the group has disbanded. What would you like each person to take with them as they go? What item, such as a teddy bear, a happy heart or a calling list, would you like each person in your group to pack for their journey? For each person in your group, write down their name and the item you would like them to take with them. Take turns sharing your answers with the group.

Name   Item

_____   _____

_____   _____

_____   _____

_____   _____

_____   _____

_____   _____

_____   _____

_____   _____

_____   _____

_____   _____

_____   _____

It's a Church Event Treasure Chest

Jump Starts and Soft Landings is the perfect resource for any church group! Stuffed full of fascinating meeting starters and touching ways to end your meeting, *Jump Starts and Soft Landings* contains over 100 ways for your group to begin and end meetings.

    Jump Starts and Soft Landings is ideal for:

New Member Classes
Leadership Teams, Ministry Teams and Committees
Recovery and 12-Step Programs
Men's Groups
Women's Groups
Youth Meetings
Retreats
Prayer Meetings and Church Suppers
Singles Groups
Couples Groups
Family and Intergenerational Events
Outreach Activities
and many more ...

Use these handy symbols to help you choose the Jump Start and Soft Landing for your next meeting!

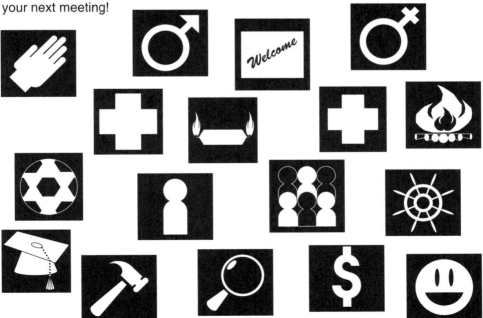

It's a Church Event Treasure Chest

Jump Starts and Soft Landings is the perfect resource for any church group! Stuffed full of fascinating meeting starters and touching ways to end your meeting, *Jump Starts and Soft Landings* contains over 100 ways for your group to begin and end meetings.

Jump Starts and Soft Landings is ideal for:

New Member Classes
Leadership Teams, Ministry Teams and Committees
Recovery and 12-Step Programs
Men's Groups
Women's Groups
Youth Meetings
Retreats
Prayer Meetings and Church Suppers
Singles Groups
Couples Groups
Family and Intergenerational Events
Outreach Activities
and many more ...

Use these handy symbols to help you choose the Jump Start and Soft Landing for your next meeting!